Joyce in America

Jeffrey Segall

Joyce in America

Cultural Politics and the Trials of
Ulysses

University of California Press

Berkeley   Los Angeles   London

University of California Press
Berkeley and Los Angeles, California

University of California Press, Ltd.
London, England

© 1993 by
The Regents of the University of California

Library of Congress Cataloging-in-Publication Data
Segall, Jeffrey.
   Joyce in America : cultural politics and the trials
of Ulysses / Jeffrey Segall.
       p.   cm.
   Includes bibliographical references and index.
   ISBN 0-520-07746-6 (alk. paper)
   1. Joyce, James, 1882–1941.
Ulysses.   2. Politics and literature—United
States—History—20th century.   3. Joyce, James,
1882–1941—Appreciation—United States.
4. Criticism—United States—History—
20th century.   I. Title.
PR6019.09U693   1993
823'.912—dc20   92-46433

Printed in the United States of America
9 8 7 6 5 4 3 2 1

The paper used in this publication meets the
minimum requirements of American National
Standard for Information Sciences—Permanence of
Paper for Printed Library Materials, ANSI
Z39.48-1984. ∞

For my mother, Elise Segall,
and my father, Harold Segall

Contents

Acknowledgments

This manuscript has had a long gestation and I have a number of people to thank who have urged it and me along. Mark Shechner of the State University of New York at Buffalo deserves special thanks. He inspired this study and has given generously of his time and expertise as it has evolved. For his patience, his acuity, his grace and good humor, he has earned more than my amplest thanks.

I would also like to thank Leslie Fiedler and Marcus Klein from S.U.N.Y./Buffalo, who from the start have balanced their useful criticism with encouragement. William M. Chace and Mark Krupnick have read significant portions of the manuscript and have also made valuable suggestions.

The James Joyce Foundation has given me several opportunities to present my work in progress at Joyce conferences and symposia, and for this I am most appreciative. Dominic Manganiello, Margot Norris, Mort Levitt, Thomas Staley, and Ira Nadel have been sympathetic listeners and readers.

I have benefited enormously from summer seminars sponsored by The National Endowment for the Humanities and the School of Criticism and Theory. Dominic

LaCapra and Wendy Steiner from S.C.T. generously agreed to read portions of the manuscript.

I would also like to thank a number of friends and colleagues for their suggestions and support: Marjorie Roemer, Ralph Kaywin, Lisa Buchberg, Hal Grinberg, Vicki Harrison, Kathy McCormick, David Stone, Sheridan Blau, Eloise Hay, and Richard Helgerson. My thanks, too, to Robert Segall, and to my research assistants, Kathryn Statler and Sylvia Linggi.

I am indebted to Prof. Jin Di of Beijing University for the translation from Zhou Libo that I use as an epigraph to chapter 1. Portions of chapter 2 appeared in the *Journal of Modern Literature* 16, no. 4 (Fall 1991); a version of chapter 3 was published in the *James Joyce Quarterly* 25, no. 4 (Summer 1988); and excerpts from chapter 5 and the conclusion appeared in *Joyce Studies* 2 (1991). Permission to reprint these materials is gratefully acknowledged.

Introduction:
The Polemics of Our Portraits

"I hold this book to be the most important expression which the modern age has found; it is a book to which we are all indebted, and from which none of us can escape." When we read T. S. Eliot's tribute to *Ulysses*, written in 1923, one year after the publication of both *Ulysses* and *The Waste Land*, we are apt to be moved as much by the gravity of his pronouncement as by the sweep of his praise. Eliot, not one given to hyperbole, unreservedly embraced Joyce's tour de force and correctly prophesied its influence on his own and subsequent generations of writers.[1] Just as he had been instrumental in getting Joyce's early work published, Eliot in 1923 contributed mightily to the advancement of Joyce's fledgling reputation when he began, in effect, writing the literary history of his generation. Indeed, in his praise of Joyce's "mythical method," Eliot himself was constructing a myth that would celebrate *Ulysses* and *The Waste Land* as the major achievements of high modernism. In "*Ulysses*, Order, and Myth," Eliot read *Ulysses* through the prism of his own poem and found in Joyce's novel the spiritual malaise and cultural desiccation evoked in *The Waste Land*. Richard Poirier correctly declares that Eliot's essay "more aptly describes Eliot's methods and ambitions in the poem than Joyce's book" (6). Implicit in Eliot's lavish praise of *Ulysses* were the promotion and defense of his

1

own difficult poem, which exhibited more chillingly than Joyce's book "the immense panorama of futility and anarchy" of modern life (Eliot, "*Ulysses*" 201).

Eliot championed *Ulysses* while others puzzled over it or condemned it. His enthusiasm for the novel was in large part reactive (in his essay, he specifically rebuts Richard Aldington's charge that *Ulysses* was formless and a "libel on humanity"), and we may appreciate his bravado even if, in hindsight, we fault his conclusions. Others—many others—damned *Ulysses* more ardently than Eliot praised it, with far less appreciation of Joyce's aesthetic gifts. In the years just after its appearance, *Ulysses* was appropriated by readers of varying degrees of sophistication in the service of one or another moral, political, religious, or artistic crusade. As Eliot suggested, *Ulysses* became a symbol not only of modern art but of the modern age, and Eliot's praise notwithstanding, it suffered more often than prospered under the weight of that association in the early years of its reception.

We must understand the controversy that enveloped *Ulysses* during the 1920s and 1930s as a demonstration of both its real and its symbolic powers of provocation. Readers praised or denounced it for what it was (as much as they could construe this) as well as for what it represented (often determined without the benefit—or burden—of having read it). It was difficult to separate *Ulysses* from the aura of notoriety surrounding it, a task made more difficult by the novel's obscurity (particularly in the years before the publication of Stuart Gilbert's *James Joyce's "Ulysses"* in 1930) and by its unavailability. American readers in particular often viewed *Ulysses* as symptomatic of a host of social, cultural, and political changes they deplored. Judgments for or against *Ulysses* frequently reflected a critic's own hope or anxiety over an age in which, as Marx had prophesied, all that was solid seemed to be melting into air. *Ulysses* became a cultural nexus over which critics with opposed ideological perspectives did battle.

In America, allegations that *Ulysses* was both obscene and blasphemous heightened interest in it and created controversy even before it was permitted to be published in 1933. Moralists and ideologues from various quarters found in *Ulysses* an amorphous but still attractive target for their suspicions and outrage. Three issues of the *Little Review*, which serialized *Ulysses* from 1918 to 1920, were seized and banned by the U.S. Post Office, and in September, 1920, the New York Society for the Prevention of Vice lodged an official complaint against its editors, Margaret Anderson and Jane Heap. In February of 1921, Heap and Anderson were convicted of publishing obscenity, fined fifty dollars, and prohibited from publishing additional chapters from *Ulysses*. It was not until Judge John M. Woolsey's historic decision lifting the ban on *Ulysses* on December 6, 1933 (upheld by the District Court of Appeals on August 8, 1934) that *Ulysses* could be legally published and sold in America.

Woolsey, moved by attorney Morris L. Ernst's argument that *Ulysses* was a classic and not obscene by 1933 standards, detected not the "leer of the sensualist" in the pages of *Ulysses* but a "somewhat tragic and very powerful commentary on the inner lives of men and women." In his oft-quoted final observation, Woolsey declared "that whilst in many places the effect of *Ulysses* on the reader undoubtedly is somewhat emetic, nowhere does it tend to be an aphrodisiac" (quoted in Moscato 310–12). Ernst had successfully legitimized the novel before the judicial authorities, as Eliot and Gilbert had before the artistic community, by downplaying the novel's subversive or potentially offensive elements and emphasizing its artistic integrity and moral seriousness. As a result, in the same week that Prohibition was repealed, Random House received the legal right to publish *Ulysses* in America, prompting *The Nation* to warn tongue in cheek against the spectacle of American "streets. . . filled with young men and maidens drunk upon immoderate drafts of Mrs. Bloom's meditation" (quoted in Moscato 7). *Ulysses* would appear in England in 1936 but would not be legally available in Ireland until decades later.

Of course the controversy over *Ulysses* in America, far from having ended, would begin in earnest after the ban on the novel was lifted. Rather than relying on innuendo or guilt by association, its detractors could now cite damning evidence from the text itself. While in 1934 Eliot declared Joyce's work "penetrated with Christian feeling" (*After Strange Gods* 48), a more typical response, especially among practicing Catholics, was that of Francis Talbot, S.J. In an essay entitled "*Ulysses* the Dirty" published in the same year, Talbot charged that only a lapsed Catholic "with an incurably diseased mind could be so diabolically venomous toward God, toward the Blessed Sacrament, toward the Virgin Mary" (quoted in Moscato 17). The classicist Paul Elmer More would also dispute Eliot's reading of *Ulysses*, writing in 1936 that the "realization of art in *Ulysses* is a creation of ugliness, a congeries of ugly pictures expressed in the speech of Dublin's gutters" (*On Being Human* 79). In a retort directed specifically at Eliot, More fulminated, "I don't see what *Ulysses* has to do with Royalism, Anglo-Catholicism, and Classicism!" (quoted in Wilson, *Triple Thinkers* 12). Controversy swirled not only around the allegations of obscenity and blasphemy in *Ulysses*, but also around the novel's alleged bent toward solipsism and despair.

It would oversimplify matters to attribute the uproar over *Ulysses* entirely to critical shortsightedness or hysteria. It was, of course, *Ulysses* itself that inflamed opinion. Eliot implied that the politics of *Ulysses* were essentially conservative; the "mythical method" was a "step toward making the modern world possible for art" ("*Ulysses*" 202). But middlebrow critics less subtle and discerning than Eliot (and far less implicated in the novel's defense) discovered in *Ulysses* a discomfiting challenge not only to aesthetic tradition but to long-held and dearly cherished moral, religious, and political beliefs. In the hearts and minds of many, Joyce, in the spirit of Baudelaire, had offered *Ulysses* to "épater le bourgeois." The objections lodged against *Ulysses* in the years just after its publication dramatically remind us how truly provocative a book this was. By reading *Ulysses* through the eyes of Joyce's contemporaries, our own understanding of the novel is deepened.

Richard Brown argues in *Joyce and Sexuality* that, among other politically offensive elements in *Ulysses*, Joyce's bold challenge to the repressive sexual norms of his day was underplayed just before and after the novel's publication in order to avoid legal challenges and broaden its appeal. Contradicting contemporary critics such as Clive Hart who continue to portray *Ulysses* as morally neutral or equivocal, as depicting, in Hart's phrase, a "morally static universe," Brown argues for the "polemicism" implicit in all of Joyce's work, particularly in its challenge to prevailing sexual codes and behaviors (3). "Joyce's fiction would have less stature, less a sense of centrality to the intellectual life of our century, less 'modernity' in our estimation, did it not respond to this felt importance of sexuality and sexual change" (4).

Brown's case is bolstered by Joyce critics who have addressed themselves more directly to Joyce's politics, par-

ticularly Dominic Manganiello in *Joyce's Politics*, Richard
Ellmann in *The Consciousness of Joyce*, Robert Scholes in
"Joyce and Modernist Ideology," and G. J. Watson in
"The Politics of *Ulysses*." While I will discuss their work
in more detail in chapter 1 and especially in my conclusion, let me say here by way of summary that all these
critics offer a portrait of Joyce as an artist more politically
engaged than detached. They agree that Joyce maintained
an interest in socialism, anarchism, and Irish nationalism
beyond the documented years of his involvement (1906–
1907) and that both the form and the content of Joyce's
work reflect a fundamental sympathy for democratic and
socialist ideas. In their estimation, Joyce was hardly the
withdrawn, complacent, bourgeois writer caricatured by
critics on both the left and the right. "His obliquity was
in the service of a point of view, an idea," maintains
Ellmann, and that idea was socialism (*Consciousness* 78).
Ellmann, Scholes, Watson, Manganiello, and Brown try
to locate Joyce more accurately in the ideological currents
of his time, while recovering some of the subversive political elements—in *Ulysses* in particular—omitted or con-
troverted by Joyce critics past and present.

Although perhaps no novel before it had been so difficult to read, *Ulysses* was not so abstruse that it resembled only an ink blot upon which critics projected shape
and meaning. Certainly, polemicists from one camp or
another used *Ulysses* as a whipping boy to express their
outrage on a number of concerns. "It is only natural,"
writes R. M. Adams, "that different groups . . . should
see Joyce under the aspect of their own particular phobias
and fixations; this is often the case of the strong finger of
prepossession at work on the wax nose of perception"
(34). "[Joyce] is a good writer," said Gertrude Stein.
"People like him because he is incomprehensible and any-

body can understand him" (quoted in Ellmann, *James Joyce* 529). Still, the perception of *Ulysses* as a threat, magnified though it was by the fanaticism and hysteria of the 1920s and 1930s, was fundamentally a correct one. Behind or beyond its technical challenges, *Ulysses* presented moral and ideological ones, and often it was the novel's harshest critics who understood these best. Joyce acknowledged that Wyndham Lewis's savage attack on *Ulysses* in *Time and Western Man* in 1927 was the best hostile criticism he had ever received. But, he continued, "allowing that the whole of what Lewis says about my book is true, is it more than 10% of the truth?" (quoted in Ellmann, *James Joyce* 596). His work was not "trivial," as some had accused; it was, he claimed, "quadtrivial." Joyce's trademark coyness and elusiveness, his impish spirit and Dedalian cunning, should not lead us to conclude that his work consisted only of unfathomable paradoxes or lacked moral purpose. "Whether we know it or not," writes Richard Ellmann, "Joyce's court is, like Dante's or Tolstoy's, always in session" (*James Joyce* 5). One aspect of Joyce's "polemicism" was to challenge in his art the strident polemicism of his age. History in all its manifestations was a nightmare from which he was trying to awake, though he would not resort to the theory or doctrine so fashionable in his time. Such a posture only infuriated ideologues from the twenties and thirties who called increasingly for a propagandistic art.

Nowhere was there more public debate over *Ulysses* than in the United States, where a highly politicized critical community often viewed with suspicion and outright hostility the aesthetic innovations introduced by European modernists. During the twenties and thirties, *Ulysses* was at the center of a broader debate about the social or political utility of literature. One's opinion of the novel became something of a litmus test defining a critic's position in the cultural tug-of-war taking place at the time. For the purposes of this study, *Ulysses* casts a beam under which we may scrutinize a period in American cultural history when polemics dominated literary debate. Since Joyce's reputation was largely built around *Ulysses*, this review of the novel's reception reminds us how Joyce's ostracism during the two decades after its publication and his rapid canonization after his death occurred against the backdrop of a sometimes fierce ideological struggle among American intellectuals.

My study begins by examining the early response to *Ulysses* among American Marxists and fellow travelers. I include in my discussion the furor that erupted over *Ulysses* among Stalinist ideologues in the Soviet Union during the 1930s, in part to accentuate the more restrained response among Party members and fellow travelers in the United States. I proceed in chapter 2 to consider the rancor *Ulysses* provoked among New Humanists and antifascist liberals during the 1930s and early 1940s. I note the irony that critics as different in taste, temperament, and politics as Van Wyck Brooks and Paul Elmer More were allied in their contempt for Joyce. Even more ironically, their harsh and reactionary criticism of *Ulysses* resembled in its fury and even in its language the denunciations of the modernists issuing from ideologues on the left.

In my third chapter, I examine those independent-minded Marxists who, gravitating toward the more liberal cultural perspective of Trotsky during the 1930s, read with fascination and general sympathy the work of Joyce and other modernists. Incensed by attacks on *Ulysses* from both left and right, Edmund Wilson, James T. Farrell, Dwight Macdonald, and others would rise to Joyce's defense. Wilson's favorable introduction to *Ulysses* in

Axel's Castle (1931) would prove enormously influential in securing Joyce's future reputation.

The polemical warfare of the twenties and thirties would not be silenced until the ascendancy of the New Critics in the years after World War II. Through their efforts, considered in chapter 4, critical attention began to focus not on the ideology of *Ulysses* but on its technical and linguistic intricacies. Although the New Critics gave Joyce's work the close aesthetic scrutiny it had always demanded, they tended to disregard those elements in it that had earlier provoked such controversy. Nonetheless, the New Critics tutored a generation of readers and teachers who would find in *Ulysses* an inexhaustible mine for research and speculation.

In chapter 5, I take up the problem Joyce posed for his Catholic readers and document the ways in which they have frequently muted his anti-Catholicism. I examine the influence of T. S. Eliot's early appraisal on later Catholic critics, in particular on Hugh Kenner, and so draw a connection between the characterization of Joyce as an abiding Catholic and his portrayal as a political reactionary. Finally, in my conclusion, I explore the dual trajectories of Joyce criticism (from Eliot to Kenner et al., from Wilson to Ellmann et al.) over the question of Joyce's political consciousness.

Although I concentrate almost exclusively on the reception of *Ulysses*, occasionally I refer to criticism of *Dubliners*, *A Portrait of the Artist as a Young Man*, and *Finnegans Wake*, particularly when the discussion of these texts coincides with or reinforces points made about *Ulysses*. Aside from my examination of Soviet critics in chapter 1 and a brief discussion in my conclusion of the English and Irish reception of *Ulysses*, my focus throughout is on the American cultural scene.

One of the more difficult challenges of a study such as this involves setting its boundaries. I have concentrated on the early history of Joyce criticism in America, opting to include those critics who were most directly involved in ideological disputes over *Ulysses*. I have had to omit or mention only in passing a number of American critics who made significant contributions to Joyce studies in the early years, including Harry Levin, Stuart Gilbert, Richard M. Kain, William Troy, William York Tindall, and S. L. Goldberg. I mean not to slight their contributions but rather to mine the rich vein of polemical criticism that is more central to the concerns of this book.

My greater regret is that I have not had time or space in these pages to extend my study into more contemporary critical debates over *Ulysses*. My book has a more limited and episodic scope, the better, I hope, to amplify and critically evaluate a fascinating period in American cultural history. But as I point out in my conclusion, some of the early controversies over *Ulysses* resonate in later debates about the novel, while the larger issues raised by its appearance seventy years ago reemerge around other, more contemporary versions of avant-garde literature or art. Current critical debate over *Ulysses* and *Finnegans Wake* once again involves disputes among theoretically aligned readers, this time neo-Marxists, poststructuralists, and feminists. Joyce continues to be a totemic cultural figure, as polymorphous, if not always as perverse, as ever. The trajectory of his career and reputation in America offers us a running, albeit implicit, commentary on the state of our criticism and our culture. In short, Joyce's books continue to read us. I offer here only one chapter in this ongoing metacritical narrative.

1

"James Joyce or Socialist Realism?" Marxist Aesthetics and the Problem of Ulysses

Until we establish an international bureau for the decoding of our contemporary masterpieces, I think it will be safe to assert that Joyce's most original contribution to English literature has been to lock up one of its most brilliant geniuses inside of his own vest.

MAX EASTMAN, 1931

It seemed that from all [Joyce's] books three values disengaged themselves, three qualities of the man himself: his pride, his contempt for others, his ambition. . . .
He had achieved genius, I thought, but there was something about the genius that was as cold as the touch at parting of his long, smooth, cold, wet-marble fingers.   MALCOLM COWLEY, 1934

A heap of dung, crawling with worms, photographed by a cinema apparatus through a microscope—such is Joyce's work.

KARL RADEK, 1934

Ulysses is a notoriously obscene novel. . . . It was completed in 1921 and published in 1922; the one person who first appreciated it and promoted it was a most wealthy esthete. Few other people have been interested in this book, where the reader, cutting through a boundless forest of words, would find nothing but worthless trifles and erratic images. Who but persons with an excess of fat would need such a book?   ZHOU LIBO, c. 1938

...but we must remain firm in our conviction that hymns to the gods and praises of famous men are the only poetry which ought to be admitted into our State. For if you go beyond this and allow the honeyed muse to enter, either in epic or lyric verse, not law and the reason of mankind, which by common consent have ever been deemed best, but pleasure and pain will be the rulers in our State.

SOCRATES TO GLAUCON, *The Republic*

Plato's injunction in book 10 of *The Republic* against the "honeyed muse" of poetry opened a controversy over the social and political implications of art that has flared repeatedly during the history of literary criticism. Defenders of the arts have been forced periodically—and certainly more frequently than they have wished—to ward off contemporaneous versions of the Platonic attack, usually with more gumption, if not more success, than feeble Glaucon. The controversy over the social and political function of literature grew particularly heated in America during the 1920s and 1930s, when new art forms and techniques were scrutinized by an increasingly politicized intellectual community. Modernist innovations in the arts were greeted with hostility by some, enthusiasm by others, and a good deal of uncertainty by many more, as critics struggled to reconcile avant-garde art with emerging political commitments. At no other period in American literary history was the question of the social utility of art raised with greater frequency and urgency than during these decades.

The very appearance of political indifference among some artists became a political issue during this period, and the name of James Joyce surfaced again and again in the continuing debate. Ironically, Joyce, with all his modernist trappings, was extremely reticent about politics in both his private life and his public art. He announced no political platform, articulated no political theory, endorsed no particular political party or doctrine. He avoided direct political engagement with all the stubbornness of young Stephen Dedalus, whose Luciferian "Non Serviam" announced his unwillingness both to sign political petitions and to pray at his mother's deathbed. Moreover, Joyce's relative silence on political matters was in marked contrast to the volubility and passionate involvement in political affairs of such modernist contemporaries as Ezra Pound, Wyndham Lewis, W. B. Yeats, and to a lesser degree, T. S. Eliot and D. H. Lawrence. Eliot and Pound were, in the words of William M. Chace, "more than interested in politics; they were entangled in, even obsessed by, politics" (*Political Identities* xvii). Often, the convenient association made by many critics between Joyce and other modernists earned Joyce undeserved scorn or praise. While he gained recognition and readers because of the association, many critics too easily assumed that these modernists who shared a good number of aesthetic practices also shared certain political beliefs. And while it is difficult to ascertain precisely what Joyce's politics were, it is easier to say with some conviction what they were not: he had little sympathy for the fascism, the monarchism, or the anti-Semitism that proved so appealing to Pound and Eliot.

Investigations into Joyce's political beliefs (notably Dominic Manganiello's *Joyce's Politics*) document his interest in socialist and anarchist thought at various points in his career, but such studies also point out the inconsistency, the evasiveness, and the superficiality that marked much of Joyce's political thinking. Although we may be unable to define in any doctrinal manner Joyce's politics, we can at least set the contours of his political consciousness from the evidence of the books he wrote. Of course, we must content ourselves less with specifics (unless we grant some authority to Bloom's musings on social reforms and utopian possibilities) and more with the general tone and direction of his political thinking. From such an overview, I believe we must concur with Lionel Trilling's judgment that Joyce demonstrates in *Ulysses* in particular a fundamental "sympathy for progressive social ideas" ("James Joyce" 46). Joyce ought to be seen as a political liberal: tolerant, democratic, pacific; nonideological but supportive of social and political reform; protective of individual liberties yet, in his own life, committed to social and familial responsibilities. Dominic Manganiello, who has assiduously researched Joyce's political interests and values, concludes that the most appropriate label for Joyce's politics would be "libertarian": "a political vision which consisted of socialism without Marx and anarchism without violence" (232). Even this broad judgment, however, clearly distinguishes Joyce from his modernist colleagues.

This breach between Joyce and his contemporaries illustrates a fundamental contradiction among those too loosely grouped under the term "modernist." For Eliot, Pound, Yeats, Lewis, and Lawrence, aesthetic principles and political and religious beliefs often were at cross-purposes. While their art revolutionized literary form, their political thought tended toward reactionary and authoritarian positions. Formal experimentation was balanced by philosophic conservatism, sexual squeamishness, and ideological rigidity. Jeffrey Meyers, in his biography of Wyndham Lewis, *The Enemy*, speculates on the reasons Lewis and his contemporaries were drawn toward fascism:

Because Fascism seemed to offer a stable society governed by a romantic leader who stopped decadence, guaranteed peace by opposing Communism, aestheticized politics and promised respect and rewards for the artist, it attracted an entire generation of modern writers who were radical in their literary technique but drawn to the new totalitarian politics: Yeats in his military songs for O'Duffy's Blueshirts, Pound in *The Cantos* and money pamphlets, Eliot (who also replaced the capitalistic villain of the Left with the Jewish villain of the Right) in "Coriolan," Lawrence in *The Plumed Serpent* and letters to Rolf Gardiner, and Lewis in *The Art of Being Ruled* and his political polemics. Despite their genius, which may have led them to create an imaginative political ideal to replace crude reality, these writers all failed to understand the most significant political issues of their time. (186)

We might add to Meyers's hypotheses the fact that the social, familial, and educational backgrounds of such writers as Pound, Eliot, and Lewis differed dramatically from Joyce's. As a young man Joyce had enjoyed none of the affluence or privilege of his colleagues. In the admittedly partisan view of Malcolm Cowley, Pound, Eliot, and their admirers "received the training and acquired the standards of the small but powerful class in American society that might be described as the bourgeoisie proper"

(*Exile's return* 115). In Pound's case, William Chace notes that "anti-Semitism came early to Pound—perhaps as a direct legacy of family background and social class, Protestant professional and upper middle class—and stayed late" (*Political Identities* 48).

Besides family and social circumstances, the superior education that these writers enjoyed, coupled with their own native genius, nurtured their insularity and elitism. Their artistic achievements may have given them a false sense of their own power and authority. They came to see themselves as cultural spokesmen and believed their political pronouncements ought to carry as much authority as their artistic ones. The boundaries between politics and art began to break down and the consequences were at times embarrassing—in Pound's case, catastrophic. As Chace notes, "Pound, who believed that the arts carry society, also believed that no difference existed between the 'essentially aesthetic' and the 'essentially political.' Poetic principles, he thought, could be pursued with little or no alteration into the political arena" (*Political Identities* 48). While a disregard for audience or current tastes may have helped Pound to excel as poet and editor, that same habit of mind drew him inexorably into the fascist camp. An allusive, highly sophisticated style that implicitly demanded discipline and erudition from the reader was transformed into an antidemocratic political ethos.

The same possibility existed for Joyce. *Ulysses* and especially *Finnegans Wake* challenged the reader and critic as perhaps no other novels had before, and Joyce seemed both delighted and occasionally distressed (particularly in the case of *Finnegans Wake*) by the problems he created for his reader. But Joyce rarely if ever used his artistic stature to make political pronouncements. "Joyce's saving quality as an artist," Manganiello tells us, "was that he distinguished, as Pound did not, between the aesthetic and the political. As a young man, he told Padraic Colum, 'I distrust all enthusiasms'" (233). It was not that Joyce was uninterested in politics. Manganiello documents the fact that even after Joyce's interest in Italian socialist politics and Arthur Griffith's Sinn Fein movement peaked in 1907 or 1908, he was an attentive, sympathetic follower of developments among anarchist and socialist thinkers. His diffidence on the subject may be attributable to his distrust of political solutions to complicated social problems, a distrust wrought of the years of violence and frustration experienced by political movements in his own country. In addition, even in his efforts to explain his work to critics or biographers, Joyce loved to complicate in the act of simplification, confuse in the act of clarification, and mislead in the act of explanation. He may have avoided political theorizing for the very reason that he could not accept the bluntness and oversimplification that so often accompanied it. His own work demonstrates a fondness for the irresolvable, the oblique, and the ambiguous that, I believe, predisposed him against single-minded explanations or black-and-white theoretical pronouncements.

Finally, Joyce's resistance to political involvement must be seen as a self-protective gesture by an artist scrupulously aware of the various "nets" thrown in his direction since his birth. He prized his intellectual and artistic freedom above all, and he viewed political commitments as the surest and most self-compromising route to artistic mediocrity. In a letter to George Borach in 1918, Joyce wrote simply, "As an artist, I attach no importance to political conformity" (quoted in Manganiello 231). Manganiello adds: "His objection to being dictated to was an assertion of personal freedom, an unwillingness

to reduce the role of the artist to that of a priest or politi-
cian" (2).

Ironically, Joyce's indifference to politics enraged critics at both ends of the political spectrum as much as
Pound's activism did. For some, Joyce became the epitome of the Symbolist and Aesthetic movements by im-
mersing himself wholly in his art. Such a preoccupation
with aesthetics was itself cause for denunciation by some
advocates of artistic "responsibility," the word that became a rallying cry for antimodernists both left and right.
Joyce and other modernists were condemned for their
self-indulgence and their lack of patriotic zeal. Eliot and
Pound, on the other hand, "were attempting to revive a
tradition of partisanship" in the arts that had been increasingly strained out of the literary life in Europe
(Chace, *Political Identities* xviii). One might well argue
that they brought a peculiarly American brand of modernism to Europe, rooted in a tradition of pragmatism,
social criticism, and political partisanship. Oddly enough,
and as misguided as his efforts may have been, Pound
was acting in a characteristically American manner in
denouncing American policies over wartime Italian
radio. His activism was in keeping with a long-standing
tradition in American letters dating from Emerson and
Thoreau. And even though Joyce's consciousness was
shaped by and anchored in Ireland, his artistic conscience
was forged in the literary workplace of the Continent,
especially in the shadow of Baudelaire, Mallarmé, Rim-
baud, Flaubert, and Proust. Joyce learned—if he needed
any instruction—that the artist disengaged himself from
political activity and created in his art a self-enclosed
world, autonomous and self-reflexive. Joyce's modernism
differed from that of Pound, Eliot, Lewis, or Yeats. His
French mentors encouraged him by their example to de-

vote himself entirely to his art and to refrain from public posturing and political engagement.

In fact, Joyce was regularly identified as an exemplar of European modernism. Certainly, it was his *art* that became the political issue among critics, not his vague and unarticulated politics. And it was in his art that critics from various political perspectives found much that was objectionable. Oddly enough, we find critics from different points on the political compass criticizing Joyce for ostensibly the same reasons.

The study of Joyce criticism during the twenties and thirties is a study in cultural warfare, with critics from opposed political perspectives agreeing at times that Joyce, among other modernist writers, was the cause or the symptom of contemporary social problems. At the heart of the controversy surrounding Joyce lies the Platonic controversy in modern dress: How does one define the relationship between politics and art? What ends, if any, should art serve? For many during these decades, art became the handmaiden to politics, and criticism consisted largely of political invective, directed at literature only as an expression of unwelcome social and cultural changes.

Inevitably, for the period under consideration, labels such as "left" and "right" to designate political orientations oversimplify and, in many cases, mislead. Political allegiances shifted quickly and dramatically, during the 1930s in particular. Political beliefs were often hodge-podges of borrowed and contradictory positions and hence much more complex affairs than these labels would suggest. In the thirties especially, terms such as "left" and "right," "Stalinist" or "Trotskyist," assumed very different meanings according to time, place, and audience. For example, it may be a misnomer to refer to some Soviet critics as "Stalinists" when many of them who had professed loyalty to Stalin were later imprisoned and killed by him under the charge of being Trotskyists. Likewise, we will understand little if we refer to Stalinists as "leftists" when, in fact, they were supporting a ruthless dictator, and their antipathy for avant-garde art was at times indistinguishable from the response of conservative intellectuals.

Nevertheless, having pointed out these limitations and qualifications, I will retain the use of such terms as "left" and "right," "liberal" and "conservative" to designate fundamentally different political assumptions and expectations. It is one of the rich ironies of this study that these distinctions sometimes blur in the criticism of Joyce's fiction. Renato Poggioli has argued that both the left and the right misunderstand avant-garde art for different reasons: the right reads it through the lens of a "retrospective nostalgia," the left "through an anticipatory and utopic dream" (168). In either case, ideology has historically served as an aesthetic blinder, with the ironic consequence that in critical practice ideological differences blur.

The intrinsic problems that Joyce's art posed to American Marxists in the twenties and thirties were not nearly so important as extrinsic considerations that made a dispassionate assessment of Joyce's work virtually impossible. What the Communists called for in their exhortations toward a literature of "socialist realism" was the creation not so much of art as of propaganda or political tracts. And the quality of literature produced in conformity with their directives during the thirties bears witness to their short-sightedness. As Malcolm Cowley confessed in his memoirs, the consequences of trying to combine Party allegiances with literary careers were often disastrous. "I cannot think of one truly distinguished work that any of them [those writers who, in the thirties, joined the American Communist Party] produced while still regarding himself as an all-the-way Party member. . . . In its general effect—on literary careers and often on personal lives as well—that venture all the way into the darkness proved to be an unmitigated disaster" (*Dream* 249).[1]

Communism was a strong lure to American intellectuals during the Depression, when old solutions seemed inadequate in the face of grave new economic problems. Walter Rideout cites as reasons for this movement leftward "the economic collapse, the example of the Soviet Union, the clarification and comfort offered by Marxism, the championing of the underdog by the Communists, [and] the opportunity for a new style of attack against the bourgeoisie" (144). Before the consolidation of power by Stalin in the U.S.S.R., the Moscow trials, and the banishment and oppression of artists that was to come later in the decade, many intellectuals who were distressed by conditions in America looked toward the Soviet Union as a model and Communist ideology as a salvational doctrine. The U.S.S.R. in the thirties was "both a reproach to America and a hope to the world," notes Daniel Aaron (*Writers* 155). More and more, Communism seemed a reasonable alternative to a visibly ailing capitalist system. Especially in the late thirties, in the era of the Popular Front, the Soviet system was hailed as a continuation of traditional progressive values that had been gaining a foothold in America in the teens and twenties under the tutelage of such figures as John Dewey. Communism, wrote Arthur Koestler, came to be viewed "as a

logical extension of the progressive humanistic trend
. . . the continuation and fulfillment of the great Judeo-
Christian tradition" (quoted in Aaron, *Writers* 257). The
great Popular Front slogan of the time was "Communism
is twentieth-century Americanism."

Economic, moral, political, personal, even religious
considerations prompted this movement toward Communism by left-leaning American artists and writers.
Many welcomed the movement as a surrogate family or
as an alternative religion, or in some cases as a countervailing force to emerging right-wing groups. The Communist party's early and fervent opposition to Hitler's
fascism gained it many supporters. But one of the
strongest appeals of Communism lay in its purported
ability to explain and remedy complex economic and
political problems. More than anything else, Communism appealed as a science that diagnosed and offered solutions to pressing social problems in the United States.
Malcolm Cowley, in a retrospective look at the thirties,
summarized the various appeals of Communism:

Communism not only furnished a clear answer to the problems
raised by the depression—that was the economic side of it—
and not only promised to draw writers from their isolation by
creating a vital new audience for the fine arts in general—that
was its professional side—but it also seemed capable of sup-
plying the moral qualities that writers had missed in bourgeois
society: the comradeship in struggle, the self-imposed discipline, the ultimate purpose (any action being justified insofar as
it contributed to the proletarian revolution), the opportunity
for heroism, and the human dignity. Communism offered at
least the possibility of being reborn into a new life. (*Dream* 43)

What is of importance to this study is the cultural contribution made by the Communists in both the twenties

and the thirties. The keystone of their literary agenda was an exhortation for a new kind of novel, one which would better reflect the needs, interests, and struggles of the working class.

> Just as literature during the years of capitalist domination had reflected bourgeois values, had attempted, while reassuring the middle classes, to disarm the worker and alienate him from his class, so the new literature would reflect proletarian values, would bring the worker to class consciousness, steel him for the role he would play in the next stage of history. Art was a form of politics; it was a weapon in the class war. (Rideout 170)

Stalin, unlike Lenin and Trotsky, set very narrow limits on what constituted acceptable literature. The doctrine of socialist realism, formulated by Stalin, Maxim Gorky, and Stalin's "cultural thug," Andrey Zhdanov, was adopted as Party policy at the 1934 Congress of Soviet Writers. Zhdanov presented the doctrine in his opening address to the Congress:

> Comrade Stalin has called our writers engineers of human souls. What does this mean? What duties does the title confer upon you?
> In the first place, it means knowing life so as to be able to depict it truthfully in works of art, not to depict it in a dead, scholastic way, not simply as "objective reality," but to depict reality in its revolutionary development.
> In addition to this, the truthfulness and historical concreteness of the artistic portrayal should be combined with the ideological remoulding and education of the toiling people in the spirit of socialism. This method in *belles lettres* and literary criticism is what we call the method of socialist realism.
> Our Soviet literature is not afraid of the charge of being "tendencious" [*sic*]. Yes, Soviet literature is tendencious, for in

an epoch of class struggle there is not and cannot be a literature which is not class literature, not tendencious, allegedly non-political. ("Soviet Literature" 21)

Zhdanov, in his exhortations to writers to become "engineers of the human soul," called for a literature that was didactic and propagandistic. Even before Zhdanov's directives from 1934, Mike Gold, one of the American Communist Party's most outspoken polemicists, had offered specific objectives for the proletarian novel.

1. Workers . . . must write with the technical proficiency of a Hemingway, but not for the purpose of engendering cheap and purposeless thrills.
2. "Proletarian realism deals with the real conflicts of men and women." It spurns the sickly, sentimental subtleties of Bohemians, best illustrated by "the spectacle of Proust, master-masturbator of the bourgeois literature."
3. Proletarian realism is functional; it serves a purpose. "Every poem, every novel and drama, must have a social theme, or it is merely confectionary."
4. It eschews verbal acrobatics: "this is only another form for bourgeois idleness."
5. Proletarians should write about what they know best. "Let the bourgeois writers tell us about their spiritual drunkards and super-refined Parisian emigres . . . that is their world; we must write about our own mud-puddle."
6. "Swift action, clear form, the direct line, cinema in words; this seems to be one of the principles of proletarian realism."
7. "Away with drabness, the bourgeois notion that the Worker's life is sordid, the slummer's disgust and feeling of futility." . . .
8. "Away with all lies about human nature. We are scientists; we know what a man thinks and feels. . . ."
9. "No straining or melodrama or other effects; life itself is the supreme melodrama." (4–5)

The novel envisioned by Zhdanov and Gold privileged content over form, simplicity over technical ingenuity; its subjects were working people and the problems they suffered; its objective was to render such subjects "truthfully," while offering a hopeful vision of a world in transformation.

The notion that art could serve as a "weapon" appealed greatly to those American writers and critics who saw the class struggle as the root of social problems. Above and beyond other purposes, art would serve a social and political function: to raise the consciousness of the working classes and rally others to its cause. Those revolutionists who endorsed such a notion were eager to prescribe formulas for revolutionary art and to denounce deviations as "bourgeois" or "counterrevolutionary." Alfred Kazin explains:

The other side always wrote of nightingales; the Marxists alone were high and purposive. Sooner or later almost every leftist critic slipped into making these distinctions; and in proportion to his fealty to the Communist Party, could dismiss—now in the light of Bolshevik arrogance, now on the strength of the seemingly unimpeachable and exclusive validity of Marxist theory—anything that did not conform, that did not point in a "progressive tendency," that could be labeled with indiscriminate contempt as escapist, bourgeois, petty-bourgeois, aristocratic, decadent, sentimental, Trotskyite, ultra-leftist, not leftist enough, and so on. (*Native Grounds* 418)

Of course, "leftists" and "revolutionists" were not really united. There was a great deal of strife, tension, and division among and within those groups of critics aligned with Stalin and those less doctrinaire revolutionists sympathetic to Trotsky. In regard to artistic experimentation, American Marxists generally took more guarded views than their Soviet counterparts. Even Communist party members found it hard to convince many others that artistic innovations such as those introduced by modernists were inherently dangerous and counterrevolutionary. Indeed, most American critics associated formal experimentation in art with revolutionary or antibourgeois tendencies; Dos Passos, much more than Joyce, served as their model. "A majority of the American writers and critics," writes Walter Rideout, "even though more at home themselves with realistic methods, praised experimental novels as attempts to expand the boundaries of radical art" (213). This may in part explain why the response to Joyce from the American left was neither so monolithic nor so severe as among Soviet critics.

The antimodernist sentiment that gained a foothold among American intellectuals on the left during the thirties had as its impetus the much more virulent reaction to modernism by Soviet propagandists earlier in the decade. Party henchmen such as Andrey Zhdanov and Karl Radek singled out Joyce in particular for harsh attack, identifying him as the epitome of the decadent bourgeois artist. Joyce's political diffidence, his linguistic experimentation, and his preoccupation with the isolated individual and his unconscious life—all earned him the wrath of Soviet critics. They focused their attack on four general areas: the formal or aesthetic elements in Joyce's art; Joyce's ill-defined politics; his general moral, historical, and philosophical vision; and the character of Joyce qua citizen and artist.

Not surprisingly, Joyce's attention to language and his stylistic innovations came under attack by the Soviet critic wary of "formalist" art. Word play, stylistic discontinuities, the search for *le mot juste*—all these revealed the neurotic preoccupations of the artist, his distance from the phenomenological world he sought to capture, and his estrangement from the reading public. His preoccupation with stylistic matters trivialized his work and disqualified him from the ranks of socialist-realist writers.

The trivializing charges against Joyce's work were common and persistent. They stemmed not only from Joyce's fascination with language and style, but also from his irony and iconoclasm. One of the earliest commentaries on Joyce was delivered in 1934 by Karl Radek (who only three years later would be liquidated by Stalin). Speaking at the first International Writer's Congress in Moscow, Radek lumped Joyce's art with "the literature of dying capitalism [which] has become stunted in ideas. . . . It is unable to portray the mighty forces which are shaking the world . . . [and shows a] triviality of content. . . fully matched by [its] triviality of form" (151). Radek's diatribe on Joyce, entitled appropriately "James Joyce *or* Socialist Realism?" (emphasis added), castigated Joyce for having failed to produce a revolutionary literature, one which consisted of "mighty pictures . . . of great consolations" to the soul of the proletariat (162). "Socialist realism," Radek said, "means not only knowing reality as it is, but knowing whither it is moving" (157). It is easy to see why Joyce—and for that matter, so many other modernists—failed to please. What Radek presented as an epistemological dilemma was in truth a political one.

Joyce was in the odd position of being condemned by Radek for his tendencies toward both naturalism and symbolism. As a naturalist, Joyce was accused of concentrating his attention on the wrong features of reality, with his work becoming morbid and trivial as a result. As a symbolist, Joyce relinquished his sense of reality and created a language of his own, culminating in what D. S. Mirsky called the "formless, meaningless mass" of *Finnegans Wake* (34). Radek set the tone for others' remarks on the subject: "[In Joyce's work] naturalism is reduced to clinical observations, and romanticism and symbolism to delirious ravings" (153).

Joyce's "realistic grasp" was acknowledged and, to some degree, applauded by the Soviets. His debt to Zola, Balzac, and especially Flaubert was apparent, for like them Joyce showed an "amazing exactness of expression" (Mirsky 34). But Joyce shared the French penchant for decadence, as Mirsky and R. Miller-Budnitskaya pointed out. Joyce, said Miller-Budnitskaya, "has a taste for depicting pathology, perversion, and suffering" that arises from a "pessimism and disgust with life" (17). Joyce's naturalism, Mirsky wrote, "has its roots on the one hand in a morbid, defeatist delight in the ugly and repulsive and, on the other, in an aesthetico-proprietary desire for the possession of things" (34). Here, the moral and political indictments of Joyce converged. Joyce's naturalism was faulted for its focus on the "ugly and repulsive," while at the same time for revealing its author's "aesthetico-proprietary desire for the possession of things." Joyce may have shown an "exactness of expression," but this precision only revealed his depravity and latent capitalistic yearnings. Words, when freed from the mooring of "objectivity," became property that Joyce, the artist-qua-capitalist, eagerly hoarded. Joyce suffered not from a commodity fetish but from a word fetish. Moreover, in his relationship to language he recapitulated the master-slave relationship endemic to capitalist society. Joyce, Mirsky wrote, wanted only to "master words and subdue them to himself" (33).

The most persistent charge made by Radek, Mirsky, and Miller-Budnitskaya during the thirties was that Joyce's work was untruthful, based on denial and substitution. Joyce wished to create his own reality through his careful manipulation of language. The style of *Ulysses* wrote Mirsky, was that of the "dying bourgeoisie, who wanted to change reality into forms of their own choice and substitute for actuality a world of forms created by themselves" (33). Joyce's "word-building," argued Miller-Budnitskaya, "is antagonistic to the idea of language as a reflector of the objective, material world" (25). The socialist-realist version of "reality" or "actuality" expressed, of course, particular political values and objectives. These critics called for a language that would "reflect" that reality, a language that they insisted should be flat, one-dimensional, purely denotative. In the socialist-realist novel they envisioned, signifier would be fused with signified; no interpretive confusion could arise.

Joyce's use of the interior monologue and his detached, seemingly narrator-less style of narration also came in for criticism. In the first case, Joyce was accused of paying too close attention to the inner life of the isolated individual. Such preoccupation, Mirsky reminded his readers, was a bourgeois affliction: "The use of the inner monologue (stream-of-consciousness method) is too closely connected with the ultra-subjectivism of the parasitic, rentier bourgeoisie, and entirely unadaptable to the art of one who is building socialist society" (34). "Joyce omits," claimed Harry Slochower, a Marxist writing in 1946, "the public character, of social time" (210).

Further, the Soviets complained, Joyce's art suffered from a lack of clear, authoritative narration. The absent narrator who, like the artist Stephen Dedalus describes, "remains within or behind or beyond or above his handiwork, invisible, refined out of existence, indifferent, paring his fingernails" (*Portrait* 215), provided the reader with too little interpretive information, and as a result no moral or political lesson could be drawn. The argument here concerned the ends of art: the Zhdanovites argued for a didactic method and a hopeful message, while Joyce, among other modernists, called for an impersonal, antirhetorical art. Georg Lukacs, in an essay written two decades later, lamented that

> modernism must deprive literature of a sense of perspective. . . . In any work of art, perspective is of overriding importance. It determines the course and content; it draws together the threads of the narration; it enables the artist to choose between the important and the superficial, the crucial and the episodic. . . . The more lucid the perspective . . . the more economical and striking the selection. (*Contemporary Realism* 33)

Lukacs here elaborated a complaint implicit in much of the Soviet commentary on Joyce from the 1930s.

When the Soviet critics considered the content and meaning of Joyce's work and tried to elucidate Joyce's vision, they inevitably found themselves in opposition. Typically, they subjected Joyce to superficial scrutiny and caricatured his positions. The Soviets sought propaganda and Joyce was unwilling to serve any master—political, literary, theoretical, patriarchal, or religious. Perhaps as a result, he was described at various points in his career as a nihilist, a pornographer, an anarchist, and an unredeemable individualist by his Soviet detractors.

The Soviet critique of Joyce was marked by a persistent moralism, directed as much at the arrogance or bravado of the man himself as at the perceived excesses of his literary style. The strongest moral condemnation was reserved for Joyce's alleged nihilism and despair, which differed so sharply from the socialist realists' enforced optimism. At the heart of the Communists' indictment of Joyce was a plain disappointment that Joyce did not share the Marxist vision of the march of history. "History," Stephen Dedalus declared, "is a nightmare from which I am trying to awake." For Joyce, history was not a path toward liberation; historical, political, familial, and religious allegiances were "traps" that threatened to enslave him. Joyce's complex and equivocal vision of the future owed more to Freud, Vico, and Bruno than it did to Marx. He tended, especially in *Finnegans Wake*, to view history as cyclical, governed less by the linear development of economic forces than by unconscious patterns of individual and collective behavior.

Besides these larger differences, the Soviets found more specific elements in Joyce's art to which they raised moral objections. Joyce's frank treatment of sex, the body, and bodily functions particularly rankled Soviet critics. Joyce was chided by Radek for his interest in the "brothel" and the "pothouse" (154)[2] and by Miller-Budnitskaya for his "notorious eroticism." Joyce, said the latter, "glorifies the principle of sex [and] enthrones the unconscious as opposed to the intellect," conceiving of the universe "as a potent stream of sexual energy pouring forth into emptiness, non-existence" (25). Molly Bloom, the embodiment of free-flowing sensuality, came in for special attack from Mirsky and a later Soviet critic, B. G. Zhantieva. Zhantieva called Molly's "'yes' all accepting, infinitely unfastidious, low, animal" (155). Mirsky concluded that "at the zenith of [Joyce's] victory he voluntarily surrendered his vantage points to the vulgar female—Marion" (34). Apparently, Mirsky was uncomfortable using the familiar "Molly" and employed the more formal "Marion" to put some distance between himself and the evil she represented. The intolerance toward formal experimentation is matched in these commentaries by sexual squeamishness and repression.

Joyce's explicit treatment of sexuality, combined with his inclusion of sordid details of urban life, led the Soviets to label his work morbid, even pornographic. "A heap of dung," Radek called Joyce's work (153); Mirsky found in it a "delight in the hideous, in pain and death . . . and a pleasure in suffering" (33); Miller-Budnitskaya condemned Joyce's "taste for depicting pathology, perversion, and suffering" (17). Joyce's desire to render a full and unexpurgated portrait of his characters was worse than irrelevant; it was offensive, morally repugnant.

A persistent charge leveled at Joyce by the Soviets was that his work was nihilistic, exhibiting only what was base and ugly. The recognition that Joyce did not believe in the Marxist vision of the future translated into an assertion that Joyce did not believe in anything at all. He was condemned by Miller-Budnitskaya, for example, as an artist who encouraged anarchism, one who wished "to turn being into chaos . . . [and] destroy the laws governing the material world and the human mind" (25). *Ulysses* was an expression of an "anarchic desire to destroy, to turn the universe into chaos, to the pathos of suicide of contemporary bourgeois civilization" (26). Joyce's iconoclasm, best expressed in his ironic treatment of characters and institutions, amounted to a revolution that was going nowhere. Because he lacked a revolutionary program, Joyce's challenge to authority and convention would lead only to anarchy.

One of the insinuations made by the Soviets was that,

at bottom, Joyce was a reactionary. Here again, they showed a tendency to lump Joyce with other modernists who were in fact reactionaries. Joyce's reputed nihilism, his "reactionary philosophy of social pessimism" (Miller-Budnitskaya, quoted in Schlauch), tagged him as a modernist in the Eliot mold. Because Joyce lacked sustaining beliefs, augured Miller-Budnitskaya and others, he would ultimately turn to the Catholic church or to some form of mysticism for comfort and clarity. The alternatives for a modernist such as Joyce became clear: the expression of a socially destructive vision of anarchy in his art, or a regression into an irrational religious faith. Joyce, like Huysmans, would exhaust his irony and be confronted with "a choice between the pistol and the cross" (Huysmans xlix).

According to the Soviets, Joyce's nihilism could be inferred in part from his creation of characters like Bloom and Stephen, who, confronted by a host of problems, seemed consistently passive or evasive. Bloom was too static a character; he was "diffident and unheroic" (Slochower). Both he and Stephen were keyless wanderers, unable to act forcefully against their victimizers, Boylan and Mulligan. Ostracized, self-absorbed, and often self-destructive, they were hardly models for revolutionary activists; they inspired neither awe nor courage. Largely for these reasons, Joyce's fiction was described as dispirited, pessimistic, "a hopeless negation of all creative, fruitful forces" (Miller-Budnitskaya 25). Radek complained that Joyce failed to document the revolutionary potential of the petty bourgeoisie: "All that appealed to Joyce was the medieval, the mystical, the reactionary in the petty bourgeoisie—lust, aberration; everything capable of impelling the petty bourgeoisie to join the side of revolution was alien to him" (180).

Bloom came in for special condemnation. A "primitive human," Miller-Budnitskaya called him, "a sort of odious arithmetical average of the genus philistine. . . in this naked abomination. . . [whom] Joyce proclaimed the real master of life, the sole possessor of the wisdom of our age" (7). Bloom's "odiousness" derived from his narcissism, the most worrisome of a host of counter-revolutionary threats.

One of the keys to the Soviets' disappointment in Joyce lay in their allegation that Joyce created characters who were cut off from vital social relations, who looked inward rather than outward for a confirmation of themselves. In the Joycean world, the social matrix had broken down, spawning misfits and isolates who found solace only in their own private fantasies or musings. In the Marxist world, one's willingness to sacrifice oneself to a social group or a social ideal formed the basis for social advancement, personal identity, and moral worth; the individual existed "in-another," as Sartre insisted. Joyce's characters lived in a social vacuum, the Soviets claimed, wholly absorbed in themselves. V. Gertsfelde, a Soviet critic writing in the 1930s, complained that Joyce, like other modernists, did not reveal "men in relation to the outside world, in relation to the past and the future." Joyce shines "the light of a projector" at his characters, "which does not illuminate but blinds. . . . He promises his audience that he will lead them to the depths that they long to fathom, but he excludes those things the penetration of which might lead to the revolution" (269). As late as the 1960s, Russian critics like B. G. Zhantieva were still chastising Joyce for "alienat[ing] his characters from reality by internal probing and depth psychology." Zhantieva could go on to complain that

Joyce portrays the human consciousness as more confused and illogical than it is in life and does not clarify, but rather obscures the picture of his protagonist's spiritual life. . . . In this way, a paradoxical situation arises: the individual, exalted by modernist literature, loses his individuality. The human psyche becomes merely a receptacle of vague sensations. (159)

For many American critics who entertained Marxist sympathies in the twenties and thirties, Joyce posed peculiar problems. In some respects, he was the paradigmatic European modernist: exiled, disengaged, seemingly indifferent to politics. Moreover, Joyce was the consummate stylist, adding elaborate allusive structures to his novels. Experimentation with language and the stream-of-consciousness technique were his artistic trademarks. At the same time, however, Joyce was a modernist with a difference. He had a distinctive naturalist strain in his writing and was quite capable of rendering a scene or a portrait with an exactitude reminiscent of Flaubert or Zola. In addition, Joyce's Irish background was petit bourgeois, and the subjects of his stories and novels belonged to this same class: lower or lower-middle class Dubliners, poorly educated, generally unself-conscious and manipulated by prejudice or illusion. Joyce could exhibit a special sympathy for victims, like Bloom, of prejudice or exclusion. These conflicting qualities in Joyce made him difficult to typecast. While on the one hand he was a stylistic virtuoso and an aesthete, on the other he was interested in the life of ordinary people, their culture, their city, their fears and aspirations. Joyce was, in short, both highbrow and lowbrow.

Such distinctions were often lost on those Soviet and American critics who adhered strictly to the dictates of the Party and tried to establish criteria for the proletarian novel. The general assault on bourgeois literature usually included all modernists and on occasion singled out Joyce. In his introduction to Granville Hicks's anthology *Proletarian Literature in the United States*, published in 1934, Joseph Freeman demarcated the terrain of the pro-letarian novel and placed the alleged concerns of mod-ernists, bohemians, and romantics outside acceptable bounds. "It does not require much imagination to see why workers and intellectuals sympathetic to the work-ing class . . . should be more interested in unemployment, strikes, the fight against war and fascism, revolution and counter-revolution than in nightingales, the stream of the middle-class unconscious, or love in Greenwich Village" (16). The proletarian novel so conceived would be neither frivolous nor self-indulgent, nor would it be overly con-cerned with technique. As Mike Gold proclaimed, "There is no 'style'—there is only clarity, force, truth in writing. If a man has something new to say, as all pro-letarian writers have, he will learn to say it clearly in time: if he writes long enough" (quoted in Cowley, *Dream* 246). Populist and anti-intellectual sentiments gov-erned the thinking of the more strident, dyed-in-the-wool advocates of proletarian literature, and no doubt discouraged many from even reading, let alone evaluat-ing, the books of a modernist such as Joyce.

But those critics on the left who struggled in earnest with the question of modernist innovations in literature often found they could not dismiss modernist writers so easily. Adversaries in the debate sparred repeatedly dur-ing the thirties in the pages of *The New Masses* and *Parti-san Review*. *The New Masses*, directly controlled by the

American Communist party, advocated a proletarian literature that adhered to Party dictates. The editors of *Partisan Review* retained a more independent Marxist orientation and adopted a more sympathetic attitude toward modernist innovations. Although a charged spirit of opposition held throughout the 1930s, editors of and contributors to both journals had difficulty settling unequivocally the quarrel over modernism.

Granville Hicks, who joined the staff of *The New Masses* in 1934 and became a Party member in 1935, is one example of a critic with Party loyalties who could not condemn modernist experimentation outright. In many of his pronouncements, Hicks did adopt a harsh and censorious view toward literature that did not live up to "proletarian" standards. In "Literature and Revolution" (1935), Hicks wrote,

If what literature does is to help us pass from a chaotic to a more organized state, it may be possible, not only to dismiss certain works as definitely disorganizing, but also to define the relative value of works that are not contributory to chaos.

What we have to ask . . . is whether a work of literature contributes to a world-attitude that is compatible with the aims and tasks of the proletariat and whether it tends to build up a system of response that will [persuade] the proletariat to play his individual part in the coming struggle. We cannot approve, for example, a novel or a play that fosters an attitude of subservience. . . . We cannot tolerate a defeatist literature, not merely because of the attitude it encourages, but also because . . . it distorts life by ignoring elements in human character and history that, for the proletariat, the ascendant class, make pessimism impossible. Escapism, too, must be resisted. The romantic satisfactions of the day-dream are recognized as perilous . . . [and] are peculiarly menacing to the proletariat. (422)

Here, Hicks all but named modernism in his indictment. The litany of sins was familiar: escapism, defeatism, self-indulgence, disorientation. Yet, in the same essay, Hicks warned against hasty literary judgments, counselling that to understand a literary work, "the important thing is to see the artist in relation to his age. . . Shelley as part of a developing revolution, Tennyson in terms of Victorian progress, and Joyce as a symptom of capitalist decline" (414). He advised against rejecting any literature en bloc and defended Proust in particular, who "left a richer and more detailed account of the breakdown of the leisure class than can be found elsewhere" (422). In an essay published two years earlier (1933), Hicks had argued that, although Proust may not have provided a "surge of determination and hope," he was "a better writer than the avowed revolutionary who cannot give us an intense perception of either the character of the proletariat or the character of the bourgeois" ("Crisis" 13).

Hicks's attitude toward modernism was further complicated in reviews that appeared in *The New Masses* in 1936. In "Eliot in Our Time," a review of F. O. Matthiessen's *The Achievement of T. S. Eliot*, Hicks attacked Eliot for his inaccessibility and his drift toward fascism. "Expression is communication," wrote Hicks, "and Eliot is saying less and less to fewer and fewer persons"; he has embraced "an irrelevant philosophy and a dangerous politics" (105). In another review from the same year, however, Hicks defended James T. Farrell's *A Note on Literary Criticism*, which was largely a defense of modernists, and of Joyce in particular, against attacks from both proletarians and New Humanists. Hicks conceded to Farrell that good books may be written by bourgeois writers and that a good revolutionary novel may take as its subject the life of an individual. And though Hicks doubted the enduring value of Farrell's book, he insisted it was not anti-Marxist: "Mr. Farrell has built badly, but it is on a Marxist foundation" ("In Defense" 109). While Hicks's remarks on Joyce consist only of infrequent asides and parenthetical references, it seems fair to say that, on Hicks's terms, Joyce's art and politics were at least as defensible as Proust's and not nearly so culpable as Eliot's. In any case, Hicks neither blessed nor blasphemed.

Curiously, however, others with less orthodox Communist credentials—fellow travellers and independent Marxists—were not so forgiving of Joyce and other modernists. Both Malcolm Cowley, editor of the *New Republic* during the 1930s, and Max Eastman, anti-Stalinist and biographer of Leon Trotsky, criticized Joyce for his complexity, his elitism, and his obsessive probing of the unconscious life. Eastman, in a polemic against modernism published under the title "The Cult of Unintelligibility" in 1931, attacked Joyce for his inaccessibility and his preoccupation with form. His charges would be echoed by Hicks against Eliot.

A dominant tendency of the advancing schools of poetry for the last twenty years has been to decrease the range, the volume, and the definiteness of communication. To my mind that statement, which has a verifiable meaning, might take the place of about one-half the misty literarious talk of the poets and the poet-critics of the modernist movement. . . . What they are doing is withdrawing into themselves. They are communicating to fewer people, they are communicating less, and what they are communicating is less definitely determined. And this is true of the whole movement, all the way from free verse to free association. (*Literary Mind* 58)

Eastman implicitly accused Joyce of "coterie writing." In 1941 this charge would be taken up and amplified by Van

Wyck Brooks in *The Opinions of Oliver Allston* (225–31). The next year, in "Literature and Ideology," James T. Farrell would accuse Eastman of having incited Brooks, MacLeish, and other critics to virulent attacks against the modernists.

In Joyce's case, Eastman expressed distress at his experimentation with language, especially in *Finnegans Wake.* Joyce's distortion of diction and syntax in *Finnegans Wake* represented a step toward the creation of a "private language"; it was a form that "finds its involuntary parallel in the madhouse."

> The goal toward which he seems to be travelling with all this equipment of genius is the creation of a language of his own. . . . It might be immortal—as immortal as the steel shelves of the libraries in which it would rest. But how little it would communicate, and to how few. When it is not a humorous emotion—as praise God it often is—that we enjoy with Joyce in his extreme etymological adventures, what is there that we experience in common with him? A kind of elementary tongue dance, a feeling of the willingness to perform it. To me reading Joyce's *Work in Progress* is a good deal like chewing gum—it has some flavor at the start but you soon taste only the motion of your jaws. (*Literary Mind* 65–66)

The result of Joyce's brilliant linguistic play would be greater obscurity and inaccessibility and further isolation of the artist from the public. Joyce would be "lock[ed] up . . . inside of his own vest" (66). He would thus be liable to the kind of caricature Eastman practiced on other modernists: "They are unsociable poets, unfriendly, and in extreme cases their language approaches that of the insane or idiotic" (79).

Malcolm Cowley drew a similarly unsavory portrait of Joyce, most vividly in his essay "The Religion of Art"

(1934), which he included in expanded form in *Exile's Return*. While Cowley conceded that Joyce's roots, unlike Eliot's, were in the lower middle class and that Joyce's work was noteworthy for its "richness" and "complexity," he chastised Joyce for "his pride, his contempt for others, his ambition." Joyce had become too insular, absorbed in his own craft and detached from his audience and the social and political life around him.

Europe was crumbling about his ears, thirteen million men died in the trenches, empires toppled over; he shut his window and worked on, sixteen hours a day, seven days a week, writing, polishing, elaborating. And it seemed to us that there was nothing mysterious in what he had accomplished. He had pride, contempt, ambition—and those were the qualities that continued to stand forth clearly from *Ulysses*. Here once more was the pride of Stephen Dedalus that raised itself above the Dublin public and especially above the Dublin intellectual public as represented by Buck Mulligan; here was the author's contempt for the world and for his readers—like a host being deliberately rude to his guests, he made no concession to their capacity for attention or their power of understanding; and here was an ambition willing to measure itself, not against any novelist of its age, not against any writer belonging to a modern national literature, but with the father of all the western literatures, the archpoet of the European race. (*Exile's Return* 118)

It was Joyce's "pride of soul" more than his technical virtuosity that particularly upset Cowley. Cowley's interpretation of *Ulysses* suggests that he did not subject the novel to close reading or that he may not have read it in its entirety. He seems never to have reached Bloom's chapters, many of which are simpler reading than Stephen's. Furthermore, Stephen's pretentiousness is undercut throughout the novel. In a comment in *Exile's Return*, Cowley admitted: "Although we had not time in the busy year [1923] that followed to read [*Ulysses*] carefully or digest more than a tenth of it, still we were certain of one thing: it was a book that without abusing the word could be called 'great'" (116).

Cowley's moralizing on the subject of Joyce's hubris only appeared to have a religious cast. In fact, his objections to Joyce originated in his political views. Cowley had never joined the Communist Party, but generally supported Comintern policies and the goals of the proletarian movement during the thirties. He wrote in his memoirs: "I thought and said that the revolutionary movement could do a great deal for writers, by carrying them outside their personal affairs, by enlarging their perspectives, and by giving them a sense of comradeship in struggle" (*Dream* 117). He had argued in "What the Revolutionary Movement Can Do for a Writer" (1935) that writers ought to take their cue from that movement and produce a literature that, in almost all respects, fit the Zhdanovite formula for socialist realism.

The revolutionary movement allies the interests of writers with those of a class that is rising, instead of with the interests of a confused and futile and decaying class. . . . The interests of my class (the middle class) lie in a close alliance with the proletariat, and I believe that writers especially can profit by that alliance. . . .

The liberating effect of the revolutionary movement has been to carry the interest of novelists outside themselves, into the violent contrasts and struggles of the outer world. . . .

The revolutionary movement gives the artist a perspective on himself—an idea that his own experiences are not something accidental and unique, but are part of a vast pattern. The movement teaches him that art is not an individual but a social product. (90)

Cowley objected to Joyce's concentration on the growth of the artist figure, Stephen Dedalus, and was disappointed at Joyce's failure to accept the Marxist version of historical process.[3]

Cowley also attacked other elements in Joyce's work that made it more private and inaccessible. He complained, for example, that the interior monologue "led nowhere [but] toward boredom and drabness." Revolutionary literature, he insisted, "leads writers outside themselves" and asks them to explore social relationships rather than the musings of isolated individuals (90). Cowley's deepest misgivings, however, concerned Joyce's detachment and arrogance. On every score, Joyce appeared to be the antithesis of the proletarian artist and therefore an object of Cowley's disappointment and occasional derision. Proud rather than humble, willfully obscure rather than simple, equivocal rather than polemical, oblique rather than direct, in exile from his country rather than in solidarity with Irish nationalists, Joyce fit the stereotype of the decadent bourgeois artist. Cowley's account of his early meeting with Joyce reinforced an image of Joyce as a frail and morbid aesthete, a composite of Roderick Usher and Uriah Heep. "It was as if he had made an inverted Faust's bargain, selling youth, riches, and part of his common humanity to advance his pride of soul."

Having been granted an interview, I went to his hotel. He was waiting for me in a room that looked sour and moldy, as if the red-plush furniture had fermented in the twilight behind closed shutters. I saw a tall, emaciated man with a very high white forehead and smoked glasses; on his thin mouth and at the puckered corners of his eyes was a look of suffering so plainly marked that I forgot the questions with which I had come prepared. I was simply a younger person meeting an older person who needed help.

"Is there anything I can do for you, Mr. Joyce?" I said.

Yes, there was something I could do: he had no stamps, he didn't feel well enough to go out and there was nobody to run errands for him. I went out to buy stamps, with a sense of relief as I stepped into the street. He had achieved genius, I thought, but there was something about the genius as cold as the touch at parting of his long, smooth, cold, wet-marble fingers. (*Exile's Return* 118–19)

Cowley's portrait of Joyce would be challenged by others on the left more sympathetic to Joyce and other modernist writers. James T. Farrell championed Joyce's work and defended Joyce against attacks from ideologues on both sides. In an essay devoted to *A Portrait of the Artist as a Young Man* (1944), Farrell concluded by praising Joyce as a "living inspiration not only because of his great constructive genius, but also because of the living force of his example, his tireless labor, despite his failing eyesight, . . . his intensely creative activity, his dignity, his daring, his high artistic courage" (*League* 59). Edmund Wilson and Dwight Macdonald contributed to the effort to salvage Joyce's reputation; Wilson, in his acclaimed study of modernist writers, *Axel's Castle* (1931), and Macdonald, in his rebuttal to attacks on the modernists by Van Wyck Brooks and others, "Kulturbolschewismus Is Here" (1941). But the argument over the value of Joyce's work and the work of other modernists continued among American intellectuals on the left through the thirties and beyond, and as long as the ideal

of proletarian art and the populist image of the proletarian artist retained their allure, Joyce's reputation continued to suffer.

It is remarkable today, long after Joyce's canonization, to
read the scathing caricatures to which he was subjected
during the thirties, especially by the Soviets. Among
many other omissions, Joyce is not credited by either the
Soviets or their American fellow-travellers for one of his
most noteworthy political gestures: the creation of
Leopold Bloom. At a time when anti-Semitism was not
only acceptable but fashionable among the literary elite,
Joyce offered as his modern Odysseus a middle-class
Dublin Jew. Bloom completed the dialectic between the
artist and the citizen, the intellectual and the proletariat,
the "hawk-like man" and the bumbling ad-canvasser.
"Joyce was the first to endow an urban man of no
importance with heroic consequence," wrote Richard
Ellmann (*Consciousness* 3). Yet no Stalinist from the thirties recognized this achievement. Only Alick West remarked in 1935 on Joyce's sympathies with the common man. He saw in the Stephen-Bloom relationship in
Ulysses Joyce's "conscious identification of himself with
the socialist movement" and found Bloom's "compassion"
to be "the socialist message of the book."

Bloom was only one of many oversights made by left-
wing ideologues from East and West in their sometimes
frenzied efforts to denigrate Joyce and other modernists
and promote the literature of socialist realism. As is
evident from the Soviets' remarks on Joyce, criticism
became an exercise in hyperbole and exclusion. The

Soviets, and to a lesser degree their American counterparts, were eagerly drawing lines between us and them,
between those promoting the revolution and those ob-
structing it, and Joyce, they argued, belonged to the latter
group. (Radek, in fact, declared that "Joyce is on the
other side of the barricade" [181].) Joyce's artistic vision
represented a corrupt phase in modern culture and could
not herald the future that many Marxists too eagerly and
too self-assuredly saw approaching. In their haste to advance that future, they repudiated the literature that
documented the present crisis.

There were, of course, substantial differences between
Joyce's social and political perspective and that of the
Marxists, yet Communist critics exaggerated these differences and ignored a great deal of mitigating evidence in
order to make their indictment stick. Yes, Joyce was
preoccupied with craft and technique, but this did not
necessarily trivialize the content of his art or deter him
from addressing themes of timeless import. Yes, Joyce
unearthed much that was "ugly and repulsive" in life,
but not at the expense of what was noble, beautiful, or
full of dignity. And yes, Joyce only tacitly supported
the Irish nationalist movement, but never gave up his
effort to understand and document the life of the ordinary man. Regardless of the objection, the Communists
consistently failed to provide the necessary caveats for
a full assessment of Joyce's work.

But the Communists were correct to perceive fundamental differences between Joyce's vision and sensibility and their own. Joyce's exploration of the unconscious
mind, his antididacticism and equivocation, and his
pervasive irony ("Joyce does not throw his whole heart
into anything," complained Alick West [126]) did not
win him many admirers among Soviet or left-leaning

American critics. Political considerations did not govern Joyce's art or sensibility, and the strong parodic, anti-romantic impulse that he exhibited in so much of his work only alienated him further from those who, to paraphrase Thomas Mann, came increasingly to view the destiny of man in political terms.

Aside from many other differences, what Joyce did not share with the Marxists was a progressive teleology, a certainty about the causes and ultimate effects of individual and collective behavior. Joyce in his work sought to preserve the notion of a dialectical relationship working in all phenomena: antithesis was wedded to thesis, affirmation was apparent in negation, and comic possibilities were inherent in tragic situations. Richard Ellmann argues that Joyce's politics were in his aesthetics, and the key to understanding how the former derived from the latter was Joyce's use of the pun. "Punning offers . . . *countersense*, through which disparates are joined and concordants differentiated. . . . The pun, verbal emblem of coincidence, agent of democracy and collectivist ideas, makes all the quirky particles of the world stick to each other by hook or crook" (*Consciousness* 93, 95). Undoubtedly—and, if we accept Ellmann's theory, ironically—it was this countersense, this destabilizing impulse activated by the pun, that provoked Joyce's Communist detractors, who were so earnestly and single-mindedly trying to convert the currency of language into political action. From this perspective, then, Joyce's aesthetics *did* carry political import, largely obscured by their political impact.

2

"Kulturbolschewismus Is Here": *Joyce and American Cultural Conservatism*

We must now become pamphleteers, propagandists—you by your own right, I as one who can aid you somewhat. Well?

ARCHIBALD MACLEISH, TO CARL SANDBURG, 1936

The literary mind of our time is sick. . . . For when the great literary artists are not voices of the people, as all the greatest *writers* have been, are we not driven to feel that they are off-centre?

VAN WYCK BROOKS, 1941

Writers must be content to hold their peace until they know what they are talking about. Readers must be willing to hold them to the job if they refuse to hold themselves. An uninstructed gentleness toward writers has been the mistake of readers in our time. Words like "fool" and "liar" might profitably come back to use.

BERNARD DEVOTO, 1944

"Retrospect brings some degree of detachment," writes
Harry Levin in his preface to the 1959 revised edition of
James Joyce: A Critical Introduction (xii). Noting the rise that
occurred in Joyce's acceptance and popularity at the time
of his book's original publication (1941, also the year of
Joyce's death), Levin muses, "Has there ever been so
short a transition between ostracism and canonization?"
(xiii). Today, more than sixty years after the publication
of *Ulysses*, when the liveliest debates about Joyce concern
the textual emendations in Hans Walter Gabler's revised
edition of the novel, we are inclined to forget the furor
that erupted around Joyce in American literary circles
during the twenties and thirties. Joyce's current promi-
nence induces a sort of historical amnesia that in its most
extreme form tempts us to believe his reputation was
given, not wrought from fierce debate. The reconstruction of the literary quarrels over Joyce in America during
the two decades following the publication of *Ulysses* reminds us how his full entry onto the American literary
stage was delayed by political infighting and ideological
disputes. We may better understand the elevation of
Joyce's work "from contraband to scripture" (Levin 240)

if we remember that it coincided with the institutionaliza-
tion of literary studies under the auspices of the New Critics and the end of two fractious and politicized decades in
American criticism.

The ostracism that Joyce and other modernists suffered
in American cultural circles during the 1920s and 1930s
was largely attributable to the stringent litmus tests applied to literature by ideologically aligned critics from the
left and the right. When Stalinist influence was strongest
during the early and middle thirties, amid calls for a literature of socialist-realism, modernist literature was viewed
as decadent, self-indulgent, elitist, and obscure. Though
independent Marxists like Edmund Wilson and those
who gravitated toward *Partisan Review* in the late thirties
challenged the strictures of the Stalinists, other forces of
reaction emerged to create an atmosphere equally inhos-
pitable to modernist innovators. The New Humanists,
whose influence crested in the late twenties, coupled their
retrograde social and political views with a moralistic indictment of modernist art. Disaffected Stalinists such as
Max Eastman, antifascist liberals such as Archibald Mac-
Leish and Van Wyck Brooks, and frontier populists such
as Bernard DeVoto also attacked the "coterie" of modernist writers. The motives and the politics of these critics
differed, but their condemnations of the modernists
sounded strikingly similar. Full literary citizenship for
the modernists was conferred by the New Critics, who
guaranteed their continued stature by training a generation of English professors who would include *Ulysses* and
The Waste Land on their course syllabi.

In the dizzying political configurations of the twenties
and thirties, it is difficult to assign terms such as "left"
and "right," "liberal" and "reactionary" to critics who
changed their positions or whose social and political out-

looks contradicted their aesthetic views. Stalinists declared themselves radicals in the political arena but were
crudely reactionary in their criticism. The Southern
Agrarians were outright reactionaries in their sentimental
yearning for the return of the "squirearchy" of the Old
South, yet they embraced modernist aesthetics in their incarnation as New Critics later in the thirties. Nowhere
was this contradiction more marked than in the careers of
the modernists themselves.

Pound, Eliot, Yeats, Wyndham Lewis, and D. H. Lawrence were both aesthetic innovators and political reactionaries. Their political conservatism often took extreme
forms: Pound's virulent anti-Semitism and open support
of Italian fascism during World War II; Eliot's muted
anti-Semitism and antidemocratic political sentiments;
Yeats's reversion to "Protestant, aristocratic snobbery"
(O'Brien 237), his expressed preference for an "authoritarian government" as an Irish senator in 1922, and his
support of Irish fascists in 1932 and 1933; Lewis's early
support of Hitler and frequent tirades against democracy
and popular or "romantic" art; Lawrence's "doctrinal sal-
vationism" (Rahv, *Essays* 275) and his embrace of "the
whole philosophy of Fascism before the politicans had
thought of it" (Bertrand Russell, quoted in Pinto 30). As
Dominic Manganiello has argued persuasively, Joyce did
not share the social biases or political predilections of his
colleagues. His diffidence about politics, the understated
liberalism he weaves through *Ulysses*, his early fascination
with socialist and anarchist thought, and his lifelong pacifism make him something of an anomaly as a modernist.
Joyce himself recognized and understood some of the
reasons for his estrangement from his modernist contemporaries, commenting in a letter in 1928 that "the more
I hear of the political, philosophical, ethical zeal and

labours of the brilliant members of Pound's big brass band the more I wonder why I was ever let into it 'with my magic flute'" (Ellmann, *James Joyce* 621–22). Yet, although Joyce did not share the political enthusiasms of his fellow modernists, only Lewis and, to a lesser degree, Lawrence, spoke out vehemently against his art.[1]

As I have indicated, the atmosphere was not so ingratiating for Joyce and other modernists as their works appeared in America during the twenties and thirties. Joyce's anomalous status as a modernist often went unremarked as critics from differing political perspectives referred to the modernists as a single, monolithic entity and generalized about them quite carelessly. Critical discourse was marked by polemic, hyperbole, invective, and ad hominem attack. A crusading spirit guided the criticism of both the New Humanists of the twenties and the anti-fascists of the thirties, fueled in the first case by ethical zeal and in the second by neonativist sentiment and war hysteria. In the crisis mentality that gripped both factions, Joyce became a convenient target, a symbol not only of the most troubling tendencies of modernist literature but of the most objectionable features of modern life.

The theoretical foundation for the New Humanist attack on the modernists was laid by Irving Babbitt in his *Rousseau and Romanticism* (1919), which traced the origin of modern artistic tendencies to the disjuncture created by the romantic revolt. "Classical" literature aligned itself with traditional forms and expressed traditional values; "romantic" literature was self-consciously aberrant and repudiated conventional forms and values. "A thing is romantic when it is strange, unexpected, intense, super-

lative, extreme, unique, etc. A thing is classical when it
is not unique, but representative of a class" (4).

Babbitt argued that modern art carried the romantic rebellion to ever more dangerous extremes. He objected to
its privileging of the private, the temporal, and the tran-
sitory in human experience over the impersonal, the
universal, and the eternal. Modern literature explored
the aberrant in human experience. Moreover, it failed to
affirm eternal and absolute values. "The weakness of the
romantic pursuit of novelty and. . . the philosophy of the
beautiful moment. . . is that it does not reckon suffi-
ciently with the something deep down in the human
breast that craves the abiding" (365–66). Perhaps the most
worrisome aspect of modern literature was its encouragement of narcissism and moral laxity. Given his religious
skepticism and political conservatism, it is ironic to hear
in Babbitt's rhetoric the hortatory tones of a Puritan
minister or a Marxist ideologue. He railed against the
frivolity and the self-indulgence of modern artists, encouraging instead self-discipline and moral seriousness. In
effect, Babbitt exhorted the modern writer to practice a
form of self-censorship, for his own moral betterment as
well as his reader's. "Man realizes the immensity of his
being. . . in so far as he ceases to be the thrall of his own
ego. This human breadth he achieves not by throwing off
but by taking on limitations, and what he limits above all
else is his imagination" (393).

Babbitt's "classical" and "romantic" dichotomization
of art formed the basis for Wyndham Lewis's savage
attack on Joyce in his *Time and Western Man* and propelled
the New Humanist assault on modernism that occurred
during the 1920s. Babbitt's ideal of classical art presented
a bulwark against the disorder of modern life so distressingly documented in modernist and naturalist fiction.

Although the New Humanists' reconstruction of the classics was as stilted and self-serving as their reading of the
modernists (a fact which Edmund Wilson, among others,
pointed out), their search for absolutes was a symptomatic response to the crisis felt by most intellectuals of the
time. Postwar disillusionment; the changes wrought by
the increasing democratization, urbanization, and industrialization of American society; the intensifying economic problems after 1929—all these developments drove
writers toward the left or the right and their respective
idealizations of the future or the past. The New Humanists, a relatively small band of conservative critics and
teachers whose patriarchs were Babbitt and the classicist
Paul Elmer More, articulated the conservative position
with moralistic fury, if not great persuasive power. Their
most voluble contribution to the literary debates of the
day occurred between 1928 and 1930, when, in the pages
of the *Bookman*, the *Forum*, and the *American Review*, they
waged what Eliot called their "tardy, rear-guard action"
(quoted in Kazin, *Native Grounds* 310) against their adversaries in the *New Republic*, the *American Mercury*, and the
New Masses.

Paul Elmer More, colleague, confidante, and ideological ally of Irving Babbitt, achieved notoriety as editor and
critic for the *New York Evening Post* (1903–1909) and the
Nation (1909–1914) and is best remembered for his pro-
lific record of observations on literature, philosophy, and
religion collected in his 14-volume *Shelburne Essays*
(1904–1937). More, who withdrew from public life after
1915 to devote himself to teaching and philosophical
reflection (one colleague referred to him as "the hermit of
Princeton"), gravitated in his mature years from a Platonic idealism to a fuller embrace of Christian theology.
Although his quest for religious illumination weakened

his alliance with his skeptic friend Babbitt, it imbued his criticism with an equally pervasive and even more severe moralism. This is abundantly clear in his critique of Joyce and other modernists, whom he addressed in a volume of the *Shelburne Essays, On Being Human,* published in 1936, one year before his death.

Edmund Wilson offers us a telling posthumous introduction to More in his 1937 essay, "Mr. More and the Mithraic Bull," published just months after More's death. Wilson's vexed account of his 1929 meeting with More, fellow New Humanist and art historian Frank Jewett Mather, and Princeton dean Christian Gauss is worth quoting at length, first for the way it dramatizes More's antipathy for Joyce, and secondly as an example of how two of the major antagonists in the literary debates of the time used *Ulysses* to define their positions.

Mr. More, who in a recent essay had allowed his intolerance of his contemporaries to go to lengths of positive ill temper in characterizing as "an explosion in a cesspool" Dos Passos's *Manhattan Transfer,* conceded now, with an evident desire to be fair, that he "recognized the element of protest in Dos Passos and Joyce." I said that, though there was protest in Dos Passos, I did not believe there was any in Joyce, and thus unfortunately deprived Mr. More of his only excuse for being polite about *Ulysses.* . . . At that time I do not think [More] had read *Ulysses.* . . . Now I was further dismayed, as it seemed to me that these three men, in their fields of literature and art certainly among the ablest in the country, were themselves disposed to outlaw from literature the greatest literary artist then alive. The same confounded old academic inertia! I thought; the same old proprietary interest in the classics, which made them unwilling to believe that anything new could have great value! . . . Dean Gauss had read *Ulysses,* but had not liked it much; and, though it turned out that Mather, the old rascal,

had investigated Mrs. Bloom's soliloquy, he would not commit himself on the subject. Paul Elmer More, who, as I say,
had evidently not yet read Joyce, began by trying to handle the
matter without heat, but when I talked about the Homeric
parallel—at the suggestion of such a fellow as Joyce's having
the effrontery to associate himself with one of the major Greek
classics—his arrogance suddenly started up from behind his
deliberate urbanity, and he sharply cut down on the discussion—(it had also been a question of whether the characters
in *Ulysses* were 'purposive' or mere passive recorders of impressions): "But Homer's Ulysses knew what he wanted. He
didn't need special explanations!" It seemed to me that there
were so many misconceptions lodged behind this remark of
Mr. More's that I had difficulty in knowing how to deal with
it. . . .

  We descended and took our leave. Still chafing at More's
attitude toward Joyce, I asked him, just as we were going out
the door, whether he had ever read Eliot on *Ulysses*. He replied
that he had not, and I told him that Eliot considered *Ulysses* a
work of the highest importance. His whole attitude toward
Eliot, so friendly before, as if by reflex action, seemed to
stiffen. "I don't see," he retorted, "what *Ulysses* has to do
with Royalism, Anglo-Catholicism and Classicism!" and added,
"That young man has a screw loose somewhere!" (*Triple
Thinkers* 10–12)

  The young man with a screw loose was Eliot, not
Joyce, though the ambiguous pronoun tempts us to think
More meant Joyce as well. (In *On Being Human*, More
suggests that Joyce suffered from something worse than
a loose screw.) Wilson, of course, baited More by invok-
ing Eliot's name and considerable prestige in defense of
Joyce's then revolutionary novel. He recognized that
More held a high opinion of Eliot, who, Wilson noted,
was "preoccupied with problems of morality, and striv-
ing, although by a different route, just as More himself

was, to find his way back to the Christian religion" (*Triple Thinkers* 5). Though Wilson himself had faulted Joyce in *Axel's Castle* (1931) for his overindulgent use of the Homeric parallel (213–15), he here cited Joyce's mythological references with Eliot's imprimatur in an effort to legitimate Joyce before a classicist such as More. But More would budge only so far as to acknowledge in his 1936 essay on Joyce that Eliot was right to have detected a "Christian sentiment" in Joyce's "The Dead." How such a writer "should have been brought to wallow in the moral slough of *Ulysses* and to posture through the linguistic impertinencies of *Work in Progress*" (*On Being Human* 70) was the dilemma More sought to explain in his essay.

More's specific criticisms of Joyce, apparent in an early broadside against naturalism and modernism, "The Demon of the Absolute" (1928), were part of a larger effort not only to deliver an ethical critique of modern art but to articulate a code of moral and intellectual conduct by which modern man might live. Even in these early references to Joyce, More objected to Joyce's use of the stream-of-consciousness technique in *Ulysses* on moral and philosophic grounds. Joyce "descend(s)" to the "lower instincts" through this technique, presenting a hero who has "no will, no purpose, no inhibition, no power of choice, whether for good or evil but [is] merely a medium through which passes an endless, unchecked meaningless flux of sensations and memories and emotions and impulses" (285). This, More insisted, was a debased and devitalized picture of man as victim rather than as master of his circumstances. The great artist offers a vision of a "higher reality" in and outside the human soul, wherein the individual is guided by "noble reason" and senses the controlling and ubiquitous spirit of God.

However anachronistic More's aesthetic and religious
beliefs may have been even at the time he was writing, he
perceived quite correctly the nature and direction of
Joyce's art and was not without some respect for the
genius required to produce it. According to More, Joyce
was by nature "a moralist endowed with that penetration
into the secret issues of life" and had a "genius . . . for the
subtleties of style" (*On Being Human* 70). *Ulysses* offered
"a reeling kaleidoscope of fragmentary images which
might with some justice be regarded as the true theme of
the book" (*On Being Human* 75). Wilson acknowledged
More's insight: though Joyce and Proust were subjects
"uncongenial" to More, he "showed more grasp of what
is really at issue in their books than most of the stuff
which has been written to exalt them" (*Triple Thinkers*
20). But while More's friend Eliot found a consoling "religious orthodoxy" (Eliot's phrase) in Joyce's fiction,
More confessed that "this spectacle of a great genius ex-
pending itself on the propagation of irresponsibility,
while the fabric of society is shaken to its foundation,
brings rather dismay and sadness" (*On Being Human* 93).

The charge of irresponsibility would become a rallying
cry for antimodernists by the end of the 1930s, although
More had in mind a meaning of his own when he used
the term here. Joyce's "irresponsibility" could be traced
to his abandonment of the "nationalism and Christian
sentiment" of *Dubliners* for the idealization of the artist
and the stylistic experimentation in *A Portrait of the Artist
as a Young Man* and *Ulysses*. Decadence lay in "the self-
liberation of the artist from the spiritual values and
dogmatic authority of tradition, and the consequent forg-
ing of 'conscience' out of the uncontrolled spontaneity of
his individual consciousness" (*On Being Human* 79). Joyce
overturned the authority of tradition—literary, moral,

and religious—and offered in its place a deified artist
absorbed in his own unfettered consciousness. To More's
mind, this was an invitation to solipsism and immorality
and a prescription for social chaos.

More returned in his 1936 essay to his earlier denunciations of Joyce's stream-of-consciousness technique,
which, he argued, not only robbed human beings of their
dignity and complexity but stripped the universe of any
order or transcendent meaning, leaving us "a world
which merely is what it is" (*On Being Human* 89). In
More's view, the dualisms that establish order outside
and inside the soul were out of balance in Joyce's skewed
interpretation of reality. The physical world lacked a
metaphysical dimension and design; sensual experience
was devoid of spiritual meaning; unconscious thoughts
and desires ruled over conscious deliberation and re-
straint; ugliness and perversity displaced beauty, nobility,
and decency; hubris took the place of humility. Joyce had
rebelled with a fury against the Catholicism of his younger years and everywhere in *Ulysses* one saw the overturning of norms and hierarchies that preserve social and
psychic order. "Obscenity becomes a kind of substitute
for the ideals of religion, a despotic faith in the horror of
utter disorder behind the illusion of decency and stability" (*On Being Human* 92). Echoing Buck Mulligan's
charge against Stephen Dedalus that he had the "jesuit
strain in [him], only it's injected the wrong way" (*Ulysses*
8), More built to a final condemnation of Joyce for offering us "religion *à rebours* in *Ulysses*, this faith in the final
reality of nature as something so loathsome that man is
relieved of the burden of loyalty to any authority outside
himself, and is left to revel in his own sense of superiority" (*On Being Human* 93).

In the figure of Bloom and the sordid Dublin of *Ulysses*

More could see only a depiction of the hellish, God-
forsaken world of his nightmares, a modern wasteland he
would denounce with the fervor of the convert he had become. His moral severity in this instance and others gave
his criticism its piquancy and power, but it also led to its
discredit and limited the range of his sensibility. Eliot and
Pound and Allen Tate, who were no less reactionary than
More and, in the case of Eliot and Tate, no less orthodox,
praised *Ulysses* as a tour-de-force and did not conclude
that the representation of corruption implied an endorsement of it. More was aesthetically blinded by his own
moral hypersensitivity. He neither completely understood nor adequately appreciated Joyce's innovations and
failed to perceive the complications and subtleties of his
technique. Cued by Eliot's sympathetic reading of "The
Dead," More could declare the whole of *Dubliners* a testimony to Joyce's early loyalty to Church and State, leading us to wonder (like Wilson in the earlier anecdote) if he
had, in fact, read the book. He seemed similarly blind to
the irony of Joyce's portrayal of Stephen in *A Portrait* or
Ulysses and he oversimplified the authorial perspective in
the latter. Hugh Kenner would condemn Stephen, as
More did, for the sin of romantic self-idealization, yet
would applaud Joyce for exposing Stephen as a buffoon.

Perhaps the best evidence of the isolation of More and
the New Humanists in the literary community of the
time was the number and diversity of contributors to
C. Hartley Grattan's 1930 volume, *The Critique of Humanism*. Edmund Wilson, Malcolm Cowley, Allen Tate,
Kenneth Burke, R. P. Blackmur, Yvor Winters, Lewis
Mumford, and others offered various rebuttals to the
program of the New Humanists. Cowley, among others,
disparaged the rigidity, the elitism, and the anti-
aestheticism of Babbitt and More and their disciples.

Moreover, he argued, their preoccupation with the individual and the exercise of the "inner check" as a moral
regulator blinded them to the social and economic conditions that largely determined human behavior and that
ought to be the concern of most writers. Edmund Wilson
submitted a more thorough and impassioned repudiation
of the views of the New Humanists, condemning their
closet Puritanism and accusing them of the same narrow-
mindedness as their adversaries on the far left. Taking
issue with More's reading of Joyce in "The Demon of the
Absolute," Wilson insisted that Joyce's characters "have
their wills, their purposes, their inhibitions, and they
make their moral decisions" ("Notes" 55). More's reading of Joyce was simply superficial and obtuse:

I cannot suppose. . . from the inappropriateness of Mr. More's
remarks about Joyce, that he had ever done anything more than
look into him, and I will venture to say that the Humanists'
high-minded habit of disposing jeeringly of contemporary
writers whom they plainly haven't read is an even more serious scandal to their cause than their misrepresentation of the
ancients, whom they have at least conscientiously studied. (56)

In spite of his many and egregious shortcomings as a
reader of Joyce, Paul Elmer More represented, along with
his Humanist colleagues, a cogent force of reaction to
modernity and to modern literature, one that would have
to be answered by partisans of the avant-garde. Moreover, he was, in his moral absolutism, at least, not so eccentric or solitary a figure as we might imagine. As we have
seen, his archadversaries on the left, propelled of course
by a very different political agenda, were making remarkably similar sweeping condemnations of modernist
literature. And the question of artistic responsibility,

of preeminent concern to the Humanists, continued to be raised during the thirties, by chauvinistic patriots as well as revolutionaries. The fervor and dogmatism of the Humanists' approach to modernist literature may be better understood as a measure of the tenacity of their beliefs and the enormity of the threat posed to them by the new literature and the new age it heralded. If we can read *Ulysses* through Paul Elmer More's eyes, we may perceive that threat more clearly and we may recapture some of the novel's original provocative power. As A. Walton Litz has written, "What our sixty-year perspective on *Ulysses* offers is not a chance for magisterial syntheses, but a better understanding of the novel's place in history and therefore a better understanding of the ways it can be read" (229).

Although the influence of the New Humanists did not extend beyond a small group of conservative scholars and diminished further as the decade of the 1930s began, attacks on modernist literature mounted as the American intellectual community grew increasingly polarized. The tenor of the New Humanist assault on the modernists persisted, even as the motives and political identities of those fomenting the attacks changed. The Stalinists' exhortations for a literature of socialist realism would be tempered by independent Marxists such as Edmund Wilson and James T. Farrell and challenged by the Southern Agrarians (whose 1930 manifesto, *I'll Take My Stand*, was originally titled *A Tract Against Communism*). But the crusade against modernism would gain new and unlikely adherents as the Stalinist influence waned, the left grew more and more factionalized, and America prepared to enter a war against fascism. The threat of fascism inspired some who had earlier been sympathetic both to the left and to the avant-garde, notably Van Wyck Brooks and Archibald MacLeish, to declare themselves American patriots and call for a literature that celebrated American values and traditions. Their purpose was no less than to mobilize *culture* for the war of ideologies which, they argued, had to be won before the war itself could be. Cultural mobilization required commitment and belief, not the solipsism and despair they attributed to modernist verse and fiction. In speeches, articles, and books during the late 1930s and early 1940s, MacLeish and Brooks accused the modernists of irresponsibility in America's greatest hour of need.

Archibald MacLeish certainly took a circuitous route to the role he assumed in the late 1930s as Librarian of Congress and unofficial spokesman for American culture. (The *New Masses* ridiculed him in the thirties as "Der schöne Archibald," America's fascistic minister of culture.) Abandoning the practice of law in 1923 to become an expatriate poet in Paris, MacLeish lived among the literary avant-garde and imitated in his own verse the style of Pound and Eliot. He was an admirer of Joyce's work, if only at a respectful distance. He confided to Sylvia Beach in 1931 that he had "a delightful impression of Joyce. . . . He is like one of those violet-breathing incarnations of the god in that sea-coast morning of the world" (*Letters* 237). MacLeish returned to America in 1928 and, like so many other writers during the Depression, was drawn into the debate over the economic crisis. He showed equal contempt for the American plutocracy and for the American Communist party, whose members he described as "intellectual terrorists" (*Time to Speak* 17), a "Soviet of garment workers or Columbia graduate students" (quoted in Aaron, *Writers* 264). He became, as Daniel Aaron has described him, "one of the most eloquent, elegant, and talented critics of the literary Left in the early thirties" (*Writers* 264).

MacLeish's association with the modernist expatriates and his endorsement of an art-for-art's-sake aesthetic early in the thirties earned him the wrath of the literary left. In a review from 1933, MacLeish offered the view that "the sole motivation of the artist is an obscure and personal compulsion. . . . For the artist is not and never can be the instrument of society" ("Review" 160). Responding to the political pressure on artists exerted by the Stalinists, MacLeish in 1934 advised contemporary writers to "admit no loyalty before the single loyalty they owe to their art. . . . What the poet must soak himself in. . . is his own time and not theories about his time. . . developed a hundred years before and in another country" (*Time to Speak* 44). Only two years later, MacLeish would sound much more doctrinaire, and decidedly more political, in his expectations for the artist. Writing to Carl Sandburg in 1936, MacLeish declared, "We must now become pamphleteers, propagandists—you by your own right, I as one who can aid you somewhat. Well?" (*Letters* 282). In a 1938 challenge to poets, MacLeish, echoing Sandburg's own exhortations, went further:

[The poet] writes *the people yes* because the *yes* of the people boils up through all the lovely images. . . and will not let him rest until it is written. And writing it he brings the mind of the nation one step nearer to an understanding of its will, and one step nearer to an imagination of the world in which it can believe, and which, believing, it can bring about. (*Time to Speak* 7)

Ironically, MacLeish had rejected Stalinist entreaties to the artist only to embrace a protofascist position that sounded strikingly similar to the Stalinists' in its call for artistic responsibility. But while the antagonism between MacLeish and the left abated when both he and they rallied against fascism (especially during the Spanish Civil War), the rift resumed late in the thirties when MacLeish adopted a more strident nationalistic tone in his counsel to writers. As his sense of urgency quickened, MacLeish railed against the negativism and economic determinism of the communists and the elitism and equivocation of liberal fellow travellers and Trotskyists. Convinced that this was both *A Time to Speak* and *A Time to Act* (the titles of two volumes of his collected essays, published in 1940 and 1941 respectively), MacLeish condemned the "liberals who enjoy the sterile and rancid pleasures of self-righteousness. . . who prefer the safety of a spinsterish and impotent intellectualism to the risks of affirmation and belief" (*Time to Speak* 16).

MacLeish directed his most pointed criticism at the writers of his day who, he claimed, were not deploying the "weapon of [their] words" for politically expedient ends (*Time to Speak* 120). In "Post-War Writers and Pre-War Readers," a speech printed in the *New Republic* in 1940, MacLeish blamed the writers of his generation for fomenting cynicism, apathy, and despair. Postwar writers like Hemingway, Dos Passos, and Ford Maddox Ford had encouraged a "distrust of all slogans and tags . . . even of all words. . . of all statements of principle and conviction, all declarations of moral purpose" (789). The effect of their writing was to "disarm democracy" at the moment when it faced its greatest threat. Edging closer to a call for self-censorship, MacLeish wondered whether "the luxury of the complete confession, the uttermost despair, the farthest doubt should be denied themselves by writers living in any but the most orderly and settled times" (790).

MacLeish often seemed reluctant to name names in his indictment of modern writers, perhaps realizing that when he did, his sweeping claims could be more effectively rebutted.[2] He would on occasion single out American expatriates and those with leftist sympathies as especially blameworthy for the American cultural crisis, but spared Joyce and other international expatriates who would appear to have been as vulnerable to some of MacLeish's charges as Hemingway, Pound, or Eliot. In his perhaps best-known and most provocative polemic, *The Irresponsibles* (1940), MacLeish seemed clearly to have had Joyce and other modernists in mind, though he again omitted specific mention of them. MacLeish's bill of attainder took both writers and scholars to task for their insularity, their detachment, and their preoccupation with aesthetics. His language evoked Joyce's: he railed against scholars "exiled from the responsibilities of moral choice" (28) and writers who saw the world "as a god sees it— without morality, without care, without judgment" (30). It would appear that Stephen Dedalus's artistic credo, "silence, exile, and cunning," represented an attitude that MacLeish believed contributed to the current cultural malaise. The target of MacLeish's scorn was precisely the figure of the artist etched in *A Portrait:* "The artist, like the God of the creation, remains within or behind or beyond or above his handiwork, invisible, refined out of existence, indifferent, paring his fingernails" (215).

MacLeish rarely reviewed fiction and on those occasions when he did critique the work of specific writers, he usually confined his attention to poets. In "Public

Speech and Private Speech in Poetry" (1938) and "Poetry and the Public Word" (1939), MacLeish discussed Pound's and Eliot's contributions, displaying some of his habitual reverence but a good deal more of his growing unease. In the earlier essay, MacLeish praised Pound, Eliot, and especially Yeats, for breaking the "teacup art" of the nineteenth century and moving poetry toward public speech and engagement with the actual world. Still, MacLeish worried that the modern poet, particularly successors to Eliot and Pound such as Auden, would not assume a position of social responsibility; there was the danger of "artificiality," of "closet poetry" that was overly satiric and subjective (*Time to Speak* 61).

Only a year later, MacLeish sounded less sanguine and much less sympathetic in his appraisal of Pound and Eliot. Pound, a "great dismantler," and Eliot, also "a wrecker of poetic forms," had founded a poetry marked by the spirit of revolt and inappropriate to the needs of the time (*Time to Speak* 93–94). Eliot's loathing of the contemporary life he documented gave his work "the cold, premeditated violence of the suicide" (*Speak* 94). His imitators adopted too readily his ironic posture and cynical perspective. MacLeish warned that "irony is a speech which can be bold without responsibility, and rejection is an attitude which can be wise without risk" (*Time to Speak* 95). Pound's influence was equally pernicious, making technical innovation itself an accomplishment and deflecting poets from their "duty." Modernist poetry was simply no longer adequate to the needs of the day, which "require[d] the responsible and dangerous language of acceptance and belief" (*Time to Speak* 95).

Had he subjected Joyce to the same scrutiny, there is little doubt that MacLeish would have found him equally deficient.[3] By 1939, the militancy of MacLeish's opinions and rhetoric suggests just how much these were shaped by his perception of the exigencies of the war effort. His fondness for battle and weapon metaphors indicates not only the omnipresence of the war but the seriousness with which he viewed his mission:

> Writing was not an ornament, a jewel, but a means to an end, a weapon, the most powerful of weapons, a weapon to be used. . . .
>   The writer-artist will. . . not. . . take the weapon of his words and carry it to the barricades of intellectual warfare, to the storming of belief, the fortifying of conviction where alone this fighting can be won. (*Time to Speak* 120)

Art had again become a "weapon," with MacLeish here echoing in a different context the metaphor employed by the socialist realists several years earlier. Amid such propagandistic appeals, the assault on modernist art was renewed, and it would not be long before an intemperate Van Wyck Brooks would add the name of the "sick Irish Jesuit," James Joyce, to the list of "irresponsibles."

    While Archibald MacLeish set the general tone for attacks upon the modernists, Van Wyck Brooks often fired salvoes at specific targets. Brooks forged something of an ideological alliance with MacLeish during the late 1930s and early 1940s drafting a cover letter for *The Irresponsibles* when, after its publication in 1940, it was sent to prominent intellectuals. Like MacLeish, Brooks surprised many when he came out so vehemently against the modernists in the thirties, since he had earned a reputation earlier in his career as a partisan of the avant-garde. Moreover, from as early as *America's Coming of Age* (1915) Brooks had been an unrelenting critic of the "masculine" orientation of an American society that was so inhospitable to a "feminine" cultural life. Some of his contemporaries attributed his conversion in the 1930s from critic to celebrant of American society to his nervous breakdown early in the decade and, in the view of Delmore Schwartz, the "brainwashing" that occurred during his hospitalization (Wasserstrom 9). Brooks may indeed have seen his own psychological fragility mirrored in the nervousness of the time, prompting him, in the words of one critic, to "adopt. . . the cause of messianism in order to save himself from disintegration" (Wasserstrom 96). He undoubtedly had a personal as well as a political stake in his staunch defense of American values and institutions against what he alleged was the defeatism of modernist writers.

Brooks echoed many of MacLeish's criticisms in his attack on the modernists, though he delivered his with more fury and specificity. At the heart of Brooks's onslaught lay the charge that the modernists represented the "death-drive" in their negativism and their preoccupation with aesthetics. Armed with an Arnoldian insistence that a social and political regeneration in America could occur through literature, Brooks blasted writers such as Joyce and Eliot ("the rubbish of our time" [*Spiller* 154]) and Hemingway and Dreiser for being eternal naysayers, cut off from the values and expectations of common people. Fascist propagandists were sure-minded and aggressive; modernists, on the other hand, seemed timid, retiring and dangerously equivocal. Yeats's lines from "The Second Coming" aptly described Brooks's mood: "The best lack all conviction, while the worst are full of a passionate intensity." In his 1941 polemic against the modernists, *The Opinions of Oliver Allston*, Brooks declared that "the literary mind of our time is sick."

These writers [Eliot, Pound, Joyce, et. al.] defined themselves
as coterie writers, and they represented the "death-drive" more
than the "life-drive", and their influence. . . had to be cleared
out of the way in order that primary literature might be rein-
stated. . . . Were they not a "dead hand," the dead hand of the
fin-de-siecle, which had prolonged its grasp for forty years?
Was not James Joyce, for one, the ash of a burnt-out cigar,
were they not all of them ashes of the eighteen-nineties, aside
from the matter of technique? And had they really possessed
the "sense of their age," to which they were always laying
claim? Or were they merely bats. . . that had flown in the twilight between the wars? (*Opinions* 231)

In this inventory of rhetorical questions, one heaped with
fury upon another, Brooks reiterated the complaints
against the modernists made by others: they were elitists
who did not comprehend the spirit of their age; they
were merely formal innovators; they were cynical and in-
substantial and stood outside a "great tradition" of literary forebears.

Brooks's indictment of the modernists rested on a
facile distinction between the "primary literature" of the
past and the "coterie literature" of the present. The former expressed the needs and longings of the people in
clear, morally unequivocal terms; its exemplar was Tolstoy. The latter showed no allegiance to a native people
or culture or to any set of moral principles; it was
obscure, frivolous, and self-indulgent. Expatriates such as
Eliot, Pound, and Joyce were most culpable, though
Brooks had equal contempt for "coterie critics" of the
New Critical school, who also were morally disengaged
and preoccupied with literary form. The metaphors
Brooks chose for the modernists were a measure of his
virulent disgust: they were spoiled children, "helpless
and supine" (*Opinions* 237), "victims of inbreeding,"

"suicide[s] of the human spirit" (quoted in DeVoto, *Fallacy* 26–27). They repudiated a literary tradition that had given human life hope, direction, and purpose: "In the testimony of most of these writers, life was ugly and men were base, and there was next to nothing to be done about it; and in fact they had turned literature into a kind of wishing well from which nothing rose but the sound of lamentations and curses. They made the present contemptible and the future impossible" (*Opinions* 96).

In the mosaic of possible political, literary, and psychological motives that might underlie the vehemence of Brooks's assault, perhaps the most compelling explanation has to do with his intense, lifelong rivalry with T. S. Eliot. He had an early and lasting revulsion for Eliot, whose sophistication and influence he secretly envied but whose manner and ideas he publicly despised. His descriptions of Eliot teem with invective: Eliot had "the face of a bird of prey," was "a traitor to America" (quoted in Nelson 239), and was "almost as bad as the Germans" (quoted in Wasserstrom 28). "I owe [Eliot] much for defining my point of view in reverse," Brooks had written early in his career (Nelson 239). Against Eliot's political conservatism, his skepticism and caution, his erudition and his detachment, Brooks in the thirties asserted his own belief in socialism, declared boldly and energetically his patriotism and his optimistic faith in the future, and reveled in a kind of cultural chauvanism. Eliot became his inverted mirror image, and in his effort to accentuate their differences, Brooks exaggerated the failings not only of Eliot but of Joyce, Pound, and others, whom he found guilty by association.

Brooks nearly always attacked Joyce in the context of Eliot and other modernists, and even in his most pointed criticism of Joyce, he seemed clearly to be arguing with

Eliot. Here, for example, is Brooks's most splenetic
attack on Joyce from *The Opinions of Oliver Allston*, one
which opens and closes with references to Eliot:

> There was James Joyce, the sick Irish Jesuit, whom Eliot
> described as orthodox, and who had done more than Eliot to
> destroy tradition. Had he not in *Ulysses*, in his "Oxen of the
> Sun," run through the whole of English literature, depreciating
> with his parodies its greatest authors, deforming every one
> of them? . . . What fools he made them seem, as he filled his
> travesties of their styles with trivial and salacious im-
> plications!—and all for the glorification of James Joyce. For
> what a big boy he must be to have put all of these authors in
> their places! The past in all of Joyce's work went out in a bad
> smell, while Joyce settled down complacently in his "snot-
> green" world; and yet Joyce was represented as defending
> tradition. (225)

Joyce was an egotist and a literary cavalier like other
modernists, though perhaps more ironic and obscene.
Yet even in his censure of Joyce, Brooks seemed to have
Eliot most on his mind. He offered his glib and rather
hysterical assessment of Joyce as a comparison to Eliot's
work and as a rebuttal of Eliot's own opinion of Joyce.
Whatever his motives, Brooks's critical reputation would
suffer for his superficial and mean-tempered readings of
Joyce, Eliot, and other modernists. And he himself
would later privately express regrets over what he confessed to have been "intemperate" remarks and a failure
to differentiate among the modernists (Wasserstrom 67).
    Eliot himself was one of a host of writers and critics
who responded to Brooks's attacks in the months following the publication of *The Opinions of Oliver Allston*. In a
brief letter to *Partisan Review* in 1942, Eliot wryly

observed how impressed he was by the "catholicity of [Brooks's] distaste." Eliot publicly implied of Brooks what Brooks himself had privately stated about Eliot: that his literary and political attitudes were reminiscent of the Nazis'. The crowning irony of Eliot's rebuttal was his accusation that *Brooks* was a reactionary—a crude and vulgar breed of reactionary, unlike Eliot himself: "[Brooks's] point of view. . . may be called reactionary, so long as we remember that reaction may move in more than one direction and to different distances; to a more or to a less civilized condition than that of contemporary society" ("Letter" 115). Eliot's remark underscores the confusion of political and cultural labels at the time. Brooks had attacked the modernists as reactionaries who inadvertently abetted the cause of fascism. He would then be attacked as a reactionary himself (by self-professed reactionaries like Eliot as well as by Marxists like Dwight Macdonald) who espoused fascist cultural values.

Dwight Macdonald's furious counterattack on Brooks, "Kulturbolschewismus Is Here," appeared in *Partisan Review* late in 1941 and elicited a flood of mostly sympathetic responses from Eliot and others. Even more than Eliot, Macdonald saw an insidious political motive in Brooks's attack on the modernists. Brooks, he argued, had adopted the reactionary aesthetic of both the Stalinists and Nazis and was conducting what James T. Farrell would call "a kind of Moscow Trial of American culture" ("On the Brooks-MacLeish Thesis" 45). He had become, wrote Macdonald, "our leading mouthpiece for totalitarian cultural values" (446), part of a larger "cultural counter-revolution" (444) initiated by MacLeish in his attack on the "irresponsibles." It was imperative for all intellectuals, regardless of political persuasion, to resist this tendency,

for its aim [is] the protection of a historically reactionary form
of society against the free inquiry and criticism of the intel-
ligentsia. It is an attempt to impose on the writer *from outside*
certain social-political values, and to provide a rationalization
for damning his work *esthetically* if it fails to conform to these
social values. (450–51)

In Macdonald's judgment, criticism had become a political act, and the politics represented by Brooks and Mac-
Leish was alarmingly reactionary.

From his decidedly Marxist perspective, Macdonald
defended the modernists, maintaining that their skepticism
and irreverence were appropriate reactions to a civilization in decline. The modernists exposed "the overmaster-
ing reality of our age: the decomposition of bourgeois
synthesis in all fields" (446). Macdonald seized on the example of Joyce to rebut Brooks's charges and advance his
own political vision. "What blindness to see in *Ulysses,* a
work overflowing with genial delight in the richness of
human life, a *rejection* of life. What is rejected is a specific
historical social order, and it is only by making that rejection that Joyce was able to survive as an artist and to preserve and defend those general human values on which
culture depends" (449). Macdonald's Joyce was not a misanthrope or nihilist but a besieged, heroic artist whose social criticism was both an act of artistic self-preservation
and a defense of larger cultural values. Macdonald, with
more depth and less truculence than Brooks, had
nonetheless fashioned a Joyce compatible with his own
politics in order to rebut Brooks's positions.

In a forum that appeared in *Partisan Review* early in
1942 ("On the Brooks-MacLeish Thesis"), Allen Tate and
Lionel Trilling disputed Macdonald's politicized reading
of Joyce while joining James T. Farrell and others in a

general endorsement of Macdonald's indictment of
Brooks. Tate universalized the protest in the work of the
modernists, insisting it was not an exposure of the "evils
of capitalism" so much as "a vision of the evils of life
which are common to all times" (38). Trilling cautioned
that Macdonald's socialism would not bring about a
"moral and literary regeneration" (47), just as Tate
argued that Brooks's exhortations in the name of democracy would fail in the same enterprise. Only John Crowe
Ransom dissented from the general opinion that Brooks's
positions were ignorant and represented a dangerous
cultural tendency.

Though voices were raised to protest Brooks's and
MacLeish's attacks on the modernists, the two were not
without their supporters. Max Eastman had savaged
the modernists early in the thirties, and even Edmund
Wilson, whom Brooks had courted for his cause, was not
entirely unsympathetic, having expressed reservations of
his own about Eliot.[4] Bernard DeVoto, who had been
Brooks's long-time antagonist, actively lent his support
to the crusade against the modernists with the publication
of *The Literary Fallacy* in 1944. DeVoto lacked the eloquence and prestige of MacLeish or Brooks, but emerged
in the 1930s as something of a frontier populist who repeatedly ridiculed aesthetes and expatriates. They had lost
contact, claimed DeVoto, with a rugged, entreprenurial
American society and had produced a literature that was
enervating, capricious, and distorting. In a review of
Malcolm Cowley's *Exile's Return*, which DeVoto termed
"not the history of a generation" but the "apologia of a
coterie," DeVoto chastised the modernists for their
"megalomania" and their tendency "to interpret purely
private bellyaches as a universal principle of evil" ("Exiles" 721). "What truly was bankrupt," claimed DeVoto,

"was not American civilization but the literary way of thinking about it" (*Fallacy* 123).

What was needed to repair this disjunction between American life and American letters? "Study, patience, sympathy, and understanding"; an "organic relationship with culture"; a literature that "acknowledged. . . the dignity of man" (*Fallacy* 165). MacLeish was wrong in attributing the modernists' problem to irresponsibility; they had simply failed to ally themselves with American society and represent it accurately. But DeVoto's literary prescription was as much an invitation to censorship and propaganda as MacLeish's. His exhortations to writers, like MacLeish's, sound stern and almost evangelical at times:

[L]iterature. . . must speak its "Thou Shalt!" as one who shares the dust and thirst. Form coteries of the initiate, turn in abhorrence from the village square to the High Place, consecrate yourself to anything which the louts at the foot of the High Place cannot know, however fine or beautiful it may be—and in the end you have only a group of the merely literary, speaking fretfully to one another in soft voices while the tides of the world sweep by. (*Fallacy* 174)

DeVoto railed against the elitism and preciousness of the modernists and called for a literature with the moral fervor and clarity of the Ten Commandments. And even though the primary targets of DeVoto's attack were the American expatriate writers, it would not be difficult to extend his critique to Joyce, as, in fact, Brooks had. Perhaps more importantly, the substance and tone of his commentary contributed to the general spirit of hysteria and cultural xenophobia out of which vituperative judgments against the modernists arose.

Joyce was sometimes at the center, sometimes at the periphery of attacks directed against the modernists during the 1930s and early 1940s. These attacks sprang from different quarters and followed different moral, political, and ideological agendas. They brought together strange ideological bedfellows. Paul Elmer More had little in common with Van Wyck Brooks, yet both saw in the figure of Joyce a symbol of the decay of modern literature and civilization. It is an irony of no small note that readers as different in politics and temperament as More and Brooks found much to agree upon in their condemnations of Joyce. In the heated atmosphere of the time, criticism adopted what Renato Poggioli has called its "subordinate task of controversy and polemic, of propaganda for or against" (150). Hyperbole and generalization combined to become its modus operandi, allowing a More or a Brooks to distill in glib fashion the moral and ideological content of Joyce's work. Joyce would be created again and again by both his detractors and his admirers, and his name and reputation would be bandied about in broader debates over politics, ethics, and art. The rash and tendentious judgments reached against Joyce and other modernists would be forcefully challenged in the forties by the New Critics, and the very premise that Joyce's work, or any literary work, contained an easily decodable ideological content would be assailed.

It may be argued, with some justification, that the reactions to Joyce by a Paul Elmer More or a Van Wyck Brooks during the 1930s and 1940s had in themselves little lasting importance for the shaping of Joyce's reputation, which occurred primarily during the 1940s and

1950s. While More and Brooks have become mere foot-
notes in the history of Joyce criticism, the hostile reception which they, MacLeish, DeVoto, and others accorded
Joyce and other modernists made possible and perhaps
necessary the shift in critical methodology that followed.
"In the heated climate of critical practice," writes Gerald
Graff, "critics tend to exaggerate in response to opposing
exaggerations" (102). The canonization of Joyce that began to occur so rapidly (as Harry Levin noted) in the forties was in large part a result of one set of exaggerated
critical assumptions supplanting another. Technical matters soon displaced ideological concerns as the proper
subject of critical debate. Under the scrutiny of William
York Tindall, Harry Levin, R. P. Blackmur, Allen Tate,
and Cleanth Brooks, Joyce's language began to receive
the studied attention which it had always demanded. And
whatever new controversies developed around his work
would take place not in the arena of cultural politics but
in professional journals and in graduate seminars.

"Great books read us," declared W. H. Auden, to
which we might add as a specific corollary, each generation rediscovers *Ulysses* and reconceives Joyce in its own
image. Our understandings of him are embedded in the
historical circumstances that demarcate what Hans Robert
Jauss calls our cultural "horizon of expectations." A historical perspective on Joyce and Joyce criticism promises
neither some version of the "correct" Joyce nor, as
A. Walton Litz warned, some "magisterial syntheses" of
Ulysses. It does show us how our criticism of him
emerges from a larger cultural brokering process on
which a variety of ideological values impinge. Our canonization of Joyce was as much an expression of that process at work as his ostracism was sixty years ago. The
plurality of Joyces created by what we now refer to as the

"Joyce industry" is evidence not only of the production demands of the profession but of the multitude of theoretical masters the colony of criticism now serves. Joyce has proven himself to be inexhaustible grist for many mills. We ask both more and less from him than did his readers in the thirties. And although their shortcomings as interpreters of Joyce are today so apparent, we might temper our judgment of them with understanding and a grudging respect for the "passionate intensity" they brought to their reading of books.

3

Between Marxism and Modernism: Joyce and the Dissident Left

The name of James Joyce is truly a collective name for many [Western writers], and not for the worst bourgeois intellectuals. . . . Yes, [these writers] are sick. But this does not mean that they are without worth. Many diseases are the prelude to health. Naturally, we must be careful not to infect ourselves. But purely and simply to turn our back on these writers . . . under the pretext that in spite of their honest inquiries they haven't found the path that is ours—, this is defeatism: and this undermines our confidence in our own power; that we have no right to do.   WIELAND HERZFELDE, 1934

Joyce's sympathy for and concentration upon the common man (who is a Jew and a target of anti-semitism [sic]), upon daily life, and upon the speech of the people, is the center of his work, and he is certainly neither indifferent nor hostile to the tradition of democratic liberalism.

              DELMORE SCHWARTZ, 1953

By 1907 [Joyce's] socialism had evaporated, leaving as its only trace the sweet disposition of Leopold Bloom's mind to imagine the possibility of rational and benevolent social behavior and the brotherhood of man. This, however, is a residue of some importance in the history of literature: it makes *Ulysses* unique among modern classics for its sympathy with progressive social ideas.   LIONEL TRILLING, 1968

I resent violence or intolerance in any shape or form. It never reaches anything or stops anything. A revolution must come on the due installments plan.   *Ulysses*

When he was told by his friend Eugene Jolas of the harsh attacks directed against him by Karl Radek and other Soviet critics in the 1930s, Joyce offered a simple defense. He pointed out that all his characters, from *Dubliners* to *Finnegans Wake*, belonged to "the lower middle classes, and even the working class, and they are all quite poor" (Jolas 14). Joyce was correct in noting what Radek and other Marxists had omitted in their hyperbolic indictments of his work. Other critics and intellectuals would rise to more elaborate defenses of Joyce during the 1920s and 1930s, when his work was attacked not only by those who aligned themselves with Stalin, but by cultural conservatives as well. In fact, Radek's own fulminations against Joyce, delivered at the 1934 Writer's Congress in Moscow, were rebutted by another participant, the German writer Wieland Herzfelde. Herzfelde, an early champion of Dada, had joined the Communist Party in 1918 and had left Hitler's Germany for Prague in 1933. In a courageous response to Radek's attack, Herzfelde defended Joyce's experiments in form and praised his truthfulness and psychological insight. While he warned that Joyce ought not to be regarded as a model for revolutionary writers, Herzfelde insisted that "he is an important writer, one to be taken seriously. We must learn from

him, as from all true artists; very simply, we must remain
conscious of the limits and dangers that are hidden in his
method" (quoted in Houdebine 44).

The exchange between Herzfelde and Radek in Moscow was only a skirmish in a battle that raged primarily
on American shores, among American writers and critics,
during the thirties. The apparent focus of the debate was
the evaluation of the work of Joyce and other modernists,
though more generally the controversy concerned the
form and content of all literature in a period of political
and social upheaval. Writers and critics with opposed
political perspectives argued continually and often heatedly
over the proper social and political function of art. What
was truly at issue was the function of culture itself.

My concern here is with those writers and critics who,
unlike those discussed in the preceding chapters, combined liberal or even revolutionary political views with
sympathy, even enthusiasm for the aesthetics of modernist art. Critics such as Edmund Wilson, James T. Farrell, Dwight Macdonald, and others sought to reconcile
their fervid, if undoctrinaire, belief in revolutionary
change with a sophisticated appreciation of new developments in the arts. Their temperament and their training
predisposed them against shallow judgments and toward
a broader, more complicated understanding of the nature
and meaning of art. Their literary tastes were catholic,
their sensibilities refined, their intellectual interests wide-
ranging and varied. Though most of them identified
themselves as Marxists, they were independent Marxists,
nowhere more so than in their literary judgments. Most
were sympathizers of the exiled Leon Trotsky, whom
they admired as much for his broad cultural sensibility as
for his political vision. For many American intellectuals
in the thirties, Trotskyism represented, in the words of

William M. Chace, "the brave dissident tradition of the left. Compared with Stalinism, and in light of conditions in the Soviet Union, it seemed to them more sophisticated, less coercive, more intellectual, more sympathetic to the arts" (*Lionel Trilling* 48). Edmund Wilson, the most prominent intellectual associated with Trotskyism, introduced Joyce to American readers with his enthusiastic review of *Ulysses* in 1931. Indeed, it was among this group of writers and intellectuals—Wilson, Farrell, Macdonald, William Barrett, Lionel Trilling—that Joyce found his first substantial and sympathetic American audience.

It is difficult to generalize about this group, whose members had no formal political association and no consistent, consensual perspective on either Marxism or the arts. There were important differences in both sense and sensibility among those loosely allied under Trotskyism. Moreover, individual views and values shifted, though usually not so dramatically as among contemporaries who were converts to or away from communism. Generally, however, what did link this group was a belief in a vital, autonomous culture, unconstrained by ideology or official control. Although they remained committed to social and political ideals, they refused to subordinate art to political ends. They understood well what Albert Maltz would realize in the 1940s: "Where art is a weapon, it is only so when it is art" (22).

In their evaluations of Joyce's fiction, these critics did not always agree, nor did they always approve. Though some attempted to generalize about Joyce's political philosophy, they were primarily concerned with his aesthetics. Rather than subjecting Joyce's art to a political litmus test, they studied its coherence, its unity, its purposefulness, its hidden meanings. They speculated about its ability to move readers and enrich self-understanding. Perhaps as important as their evaluation of Joyce's art was their enunciation of a cultural perspective that was tolerant, flexible, and broad-minded. Whatever Joyce's particular merits or demerits, he would be read seriously, as would other modernists, indeed, as would any writer who conscientiously applied himself to his discipline. Through their efforts, these critics sustained what Lionel Trilling would later call "the primal imagination of liberalism": the "imagination of variousness and possibility, which implies the awareness of complexity and difficulty" (*Liberal Imagination* xii). They sought to preserve the kind of rich and diverse culture that allowed an experimental writer such as Joyce—or any of the artistic sons and daughters he fathered—to flourish.

Trotsky served as both a martyr and a model to those American writers and critics who came to be referred to as Trotskyists. Trotsky provided them with a rationale for favoring modernist literature over the literature of socialist realism, much of which was written under the auspices of the Communist party. And he did so without making these critics feel they were abandoning the principles or goals of the socialist revolution. Trotsky "very clearly perceived the theoretical and practical weaknesses in the concept of proletarian art, literature, and culture" (Wilson, "Marxism" 273). His key contention was that the emergent proletarian class had not produced and would not produce a literature of its own, since the dictatorship of the proletariat was to be only a transitional phase which would one day create "a culture which is

above classes and which will be the first truly human culture" (quoted in Wilson, "Marxism" 272). In the mean-
time, Trotsky argued, "such terms as 'proletarian literature' and 'proletarian culture' are dangerous, because they
erroneously compress the culture of the future into the
narrow limits of the present day" (*Literature and Art* 37).

Trotsky argued against the intervention of revolutionary leaders or theoreticians in the artistic arena. "Art must
make its own way by its own means," he declared. "The
domain of art is not one in which the Party is called upon
to command" (*Literature and Art* 19). Trotsky displayed
an understanding of the artistic process and a respect for
artistic purposes that, he implored, should not be manipulated for narrow political ends. He protested adamantly
against the controls imposed on Soviet literature by
Stalin, complaining that the Stalinist bureaucracy produced only sycophancy and mediocrity.

Trotsky's contribution lay in his ability to separate
artistic judgments from political ones. His was "an
ideologically but not culturally orthodox mind," in the
words of Renato Poggioli. Max Eastman, who along
with many others retreated from Stalinist communism in
the late twenties and early thirties, admired Trotsky's
artistic tolerance. Trotsky and Lenin, Eastman argued in
Artists in Uniform, made a critical distinction between the
revolutionary process and the creative process:

They both were wise enough instinctively to feel that a philosophy which "conceives reality" in the form of practical procedure towards a goal, can not give directives to creative art,
which *perceives* reality and carries a goal within itself. . . . It
was thus by relaxing or "putting in its place" the dialectic
metaphysic, that Lenin and Trotsky managed a wise attitude to
artists and their problems. (37)

Trotsky was unwilling to dismiss bourgeois literature, or any other literature that was not overtly counterrevolutionary. Wrote Trotsky: "One cannot always go to the principles of Marxism in deciding whether to accept or reject a work of art" (quoted in Wilson, "Marxism" 273). Any literature, even that written by an elite, aristocratic class, could be educative, if indeed it was *good* literature. And even seemingly trivial or innocuous texts could prove to be profound or subversive on close examination. Trotsky refused to be a cultural policeman.

> It is childish to think that bourgeois belles lettres can make a breach in class solidarity. What the worker will take from Shakespeare, Goethe, Pushkin, or Dostoevsky, will be a more complex idea of human personality, of its passions and feelings, a deeper and profounder understanding of its psychic forces and of the role of the subconscious. . . . In the final analysis, the worker will be richer. (*Literature and Revolution* 225)

It is not difficult to see how Trotsky's position, as it gained greater influence over critical opinion in America, created a cultural milieu in which James Joyce's work could be seriously considered.

James T. Farrell, though not the most eloquent, was perhaps the most boisterous spokesman for that faction among American writers and critics loosely allied with Trotsky. In his biography of Farrell, Alan Wald refers to him as a "paradigmatic" Trotskyist: "He embodied many representative qualities of the Trotskyist intellectuals and became one of their central organizers and spokesmen" (4). Indeed, many of Farrell's warnings and exhortations delivered in the thirties and forties echo his and Trotsky's contemporaries Wilson, Rahv, and Macdonald. He supported Comintern efforts to create a proletarian literature early in the thirties and was selected for inclusion in Granville Hicks's anthology *Proletarian Literature in the United States,* published in 1935. But he soon moved away from the Party and the movement for proletarian literature, inveighing against the "ideological policemen" of both the left and right. His career was marked by his sometimes bristling contentiousness, his consistent denunciations of political interference in literary affairs, and his enduring respect for the life and art of James Joyce. His defenses of Joyce illustrate well his positions in the ideological debates of his day.

In *A Note on Literary Criticism* (1936), Farrell refuted the charges made against Joyce by Karl Radek and D. S. Mirsky, calling them "irrelevant and unreasonable." Farrell defended Joyce's explicit realism, his stream-of-consciousness technique, his fascination with the life of the common man. He protested Radek's dismissal of *Ulysses* as bourgeois art, arguing that "proletarian" and "bourgeois" were not normative but descriptive terms. Moreover, he reminded Radek, Joyce's antagonism to both Church and State certainly made him an atypical bourgeois, one, he implied, with more socialistic sympathies than Radek granted. Finally, Farrell applauded Joyce's use of the "urban landscape" in *Ulysses,* suggesting that it might serve as a model for other Irish writers, "one of whom," he sarcastically intoned, "may write a book to satisfy Radek's thesis of social realism."

With the publication of *A Note on Literary Criticism,* Farrell effectively severed his ties with the Communist party and moved closer philosophically to Philip Rahv and William Phillips of the newly founded *Partisan Re-*

view. In his book, Farrell acknowledged the importance of a literary tradition, expressed his opposition to mechanistic applications of Marxism to literature, and defended the technical innovations introduced by Joyce and other modernists. "Written at a polemical heat" (Calmer 7), *A Note on Literary Criticism* attacked the oversimplifications of Marxist criticism and the anti-aestheticism of proletarian literature. Literature, Farrell argued, could not be fairly evaluated on the grounds of social utility. Farrell would write in 1942: "Literature . . . cannot, in and of itself, solve social and political problems. Any solution of a social or political problem in a work of literature is a purely intellectual solution" (quoted in Wald 115).

Much of Farrell's most impassioned, and at times vitriolic criticism was written in response to polemical broadsides from both Stalinists and cultural conservatives. James Joyce's name came up continually in the arguments that raged during the thirties, and Farrell's contributions to the debates are both explicit and implicit defenses of Joyce and other modernists. Farrell defended Joyce explicitly in *A Note on Literary Criticism* against the attacks by Radek and others on the Stalinist left. When modernism was attacked by Van Wyck Brooks and Archibald MacLeish, Farrell responded in 1944 with a collection of essays entitled *The League of Frightened Philistines*. Here again, he placed specific praise of Joyce (in "Joyce's *A Portrait of the Artist as a Young Man*") alongside militant theoretical counterattacks against Brooks and other cultural conservatives.

Brooks and MacLeish, Farrell pointed out, owed much of their reactionary perspective to the New Humanists who had preceded them, namely Babbitt and More. These "frightened Philistines," as Farrell called Brooks and MacLeish, attacked both the naturalists and the avant-garde for their realistic, often critical portrayals of contemporary society. "Both realists and avant-garde writers have written in a kind of warning, a warning that much is wrong, morally wrong in this world," wrote Farrell. "Advance guard writers of our era . . . have expressed the doubts, the anguishes, the agonies in the psyche of man" (*League* 9). The new moralists wished only that modern literature could "hide away in a hot-house," avoiding the problems of contemporary life and taking solace in the values and customs of the past. But, Farrell argued, literature must be directly and honestly engaged with human experience, and the experience of modern life is often one of chaos and disorder. Modern art must be wary of the chauvinism, the sentimentality, and the moral absolutism proffered by the New Humanists.

MacLeish and Brooks edge closer to literary prescription in their calls for a "responsible" literature, and they are as guilty as the Stalinists of efforts to politicize art.

In essence, Brooks is adopting the same general attitude toward literature as did his recent forebears, the apostles of proletarian literature, even though he clothes his views in a concealing dress of moralism. Like them, he and MacLeish and others are seeking to legislate for writing, to tell the writer what to do, what to write, what ideology to inculcate through his works, what conclusions to come to in a novel, and what to think. ("Literature" 95–6)

Straining toward a higher note of melodrama, Farrell finally accused these "shepherds of the status quo" of contributing to the mobilization of American society for war: "they are involved as part of a general metaphysics of the war" (92).

In the essay on Joyce collected in *The League of Frightened Philistines*, Farrell reiterated much of what he had earlier said about *A Portrait* and made brief but admiring comments on both *Ulysses* and *Finnegans Wake*. He lionized Stephen Dedalus, the alienated artist who, Farrell blithely predicted, *will* forge the conscience of his race and help his people "become more noble" (58). Even from the vantage point post-*Ulysses*, Farrell saw none of the irony in Joyce's characterization of Stephen. He romanticized Stephen, the epitome of the alienated modern artist, as ardently as his adversaries on the left and the right lampooned him. In his impassioned defense of Stephen, Farrell was again arguing in defense of Joyce. Similarly, in his laudatory portrait of Joyce the artist, Farrell seemed eager to dispel the image, advanced throughout the 1930s, of Joyce as decadent and neurotic. Besides Stalinists and conservatives, Max Eastman and Malcolm Cowley had contributed portraits of Joyce that reinforced this image (Eastman in "The Cult of Unintelligibility" in 1931, Cowley in "The Religion of Art" in 1934). Eastman had referred to Joyce and his modernist ilk as "uncommunicative" and "unfriendly"; Cowley had called Joyce an "inhuman and cold genius." Characteristically, Farrell offered his rebuttal:[1]

[Joyce] remains in literature a living inspiration not only because of his great constructive genius, but also because of the living force of his example, his tireless labor, despite his failing eyesight, on major projects, his intensely creative activity, his dignity, his daring, his high artistic courage. Great as is his influence upon the technique of his art, that of his very example is likely to be equally important on writers of the future. (59)

Farrell's comments on Joyce were often dissonant echoes of the opinions of Edmund Wilson, the most eloquent and influential among those critics sympathetic to Trotsky. More assiduously and more convincingly than other critics of the time, Wilson attempted to reconcile what he viewed as the most dynamic and progressive forces in politics and art: Marxism and modernism. He embraced neither uncritically or unambivalently, but persisted in the belief that a revolutionary art was neither the inherent cause nor the effect of a counterrevolutionary politics. He remained stubbornly independent in his literary judgments, beholden to the dogmas of neither the left nor the right: Paul Elmer More, he declared, was as wrongheaded in his literary judgments as Upton Sinclair. "Each insists on denouncing as irresponsible and evil or futile all the writers in which it is impossible for him to find his own particular moral stated in his own particular terms" ("Notes" 461).

Wilson occupied a rather anomalous position among the writers and critics of his day. He was occasionally involved in the activities of the American Communist Party at the same time that he was preparing the manuscript of *Axel's Castle*, in which he promoted the work of Joyce and other modernists whom most Stalinists had branded decadent and bourgeois. Moreover, Wilson's genteel family background and highbrow Princeton education were credentials more likely to place him in the camp of Babbitt's New Humanists than in the American Communist Party of Mike Gold and Waldo Frank. The left regarded him as an important catch who might bring other

middle-class writers into its ranks. Clifton Fadiman referred to Wilson as a "potentially important personality
in the revolutionary movement. . . splendidly equipped
to open the eyes of those members of his own class who
are lagging behind" (quoted in Aaron, "Wilson's Decade"
177–78).

Indeed, Wilson, along with many others, became increasingly disillusioned with capitalist society and, as the
thirties began, edged closer to affiliation with those "convinced and cool-headed revolutionists" (quoted in Aaron,
"Wilson's Decade" 175) who looked to Russia for hope
and direction. *The American Jitters* (1932), his chronicle of
the strikes, riots, and trials of depression-era America,
convinced many that Wilson himself had crossed the barricade. He railed against the injustices of a class society
and the complacency that underlay it. Though he did not
advocate a proletarian culture, he showed general sympathy for Party efforts to fashion a literature more re-
sponsive to the struggles and aspirations of the common
man. Socialism, he believed, could profoundly alter
American culture, "in form and style. . . as well as in
point of view" (quoted in Aaron, *Writers* 252).

Wilson's increasing interest and involvement in the
activities of the left was reflected in his literary judgments
at the time, particularly in his misgivings about some of
the tendencies of modernist art. Although he was preparing a generally sympathetic introduction of Joyce, Proust,
Eliot, Valéry, and others in *Axel's Castle*, he confessed to
Christian Gauss in November, 1929 that his steady "diet
of Symbolism" had had the effect of "wearying and
almost disgusting me": "I have a feeling that [Symbol-
ism] has about run its course, and hope to see its dis-
coveries in psychology and language taken over by some

different artistic tendency" (*Letters* 177–78). A year earlier, he had voiced even more profound misgivings about
the modernists and included Joyce in his general indictment of their subjectivism:

Now I consider. . . Yeats, Proust, and Joyce. . . among the
greatest in modern literature, and even now, not half enough
appreciated. . . . But they are themselves. . . open to serious
criticism. In every one of them, the emphasis on contempla-
tion, on the study of the individual soul—or rather, the individual mind, as in Valery's case, the individual temperament, as
in Proust's, the individual "stream of consciousness," as in
Joyce—has led to a kind of resignation in regard to the world at
large, in fact, to that discouragement of the will of which Yeats
is always talking. . . . The heroes of these writers never act on
their fellows, their thoughts never pass into action. (*Letters*
150–51)

Wilson's criticisms here sound strikingly similar to those
that would be delivered by Stalinists and New Humanists
during the thirties.

Yet, when Wilson was drawn into public debate over
the contribution of the modernists, he consistently defended them against the attacks from the literary left and
right. Wilson bristled at the intolerance of both sides,
fueled on the left by political dogmatism and on the right
by moral prudery and a reflexive distrust of the new.
When More condemned Joyce's use of the stream-of-
consciousness technique for the passivity it induced in his
characters—a charge Wilson himself had made privately
only two years earlier—Wilson, without equivocation,
replied that he was wrong. "[Joyce's] characters are all
going about their business like the characters of any other
novelist. Bloom, Dedalus, Mrs. Bloom and others do

have their wills, their purposes, their inhibitions, and
they make their moral decisions—indeed, these moral decisions are the crucial events of *Ulysses*" ("Notes" 463).
Wilson's public pronouncements bore scant evidence of
his private doubts. Caught up in the increasingly acrimo-
nious debate over modernism, Wilson emerged as a partisan of the avant-garde and more generally as an irrepressible advocate of artistic freedom and cultural
diversity.

Although he was sympathetic to the left in the late
1920s, Wilson had always demonstrated his independence
from the Party organization and many of its policies and,
along with Farrell and others, distanced himself further as
the decade of the 1930s progressed. He remained, in the
words of Daniel Aaron, "intellectually unsubmissive,"
critical of the excesses and distortions emanating from
both the left and the right. His literary judgments were
marked by a scholar's erudition and detachment, an
historian's sense of cultural tradition, an artist's appreciation for nuance and technique, and a minister's "moral
gravity."[2] The latter gave his literary opinions a particular
resonance and power and reinforced his authority as a
cultural spokesman.

Wilson's stature and eloquence lent weight to his literary opinions, no more so than in his favorable assessment
of *Ulysses*, which appeared in *Axel's Castle* in 1931. Wilson's essay is a crucial document in the history of Joyce
criticism. For many Americans, it introduced a writer
whose principal work had been banned for the nine years
since its publication. More importantly, Wilson presented
an enthusiastic yet balanced reading of Joyce, in sharp
contrast to the harsh and hyperbolic criticism he had received from the Humanists and the Stalinists. Wilson,
more effectively than Farrell, redeemed Joyce's reputation

for an American audience that would become Joyce's largest and most devoted. In so doing, Wilson, like Farrell, implicitly used Joyce to prepare a case that he would later present against ideologues from both the left and the right. Wilson would refine his arguments against the strict application of Marxist theory to literature in an essay that appeared in a 1938 collection, *The Triple Thinkers*. In "Marxism and Literature," Wilson criticized efforts of both the left and right to prescribe suitable subjects and themes for literature. More thorough, more reasoned, and less truculent than Farrell, Wilson argued that literary works were morally and thematically complex, not suited for the task of "pamphleteering" that so many wished literature to perform.

It is usually true in works of the highest order that the purport is not a simple message, but a complex vision of things, which itself is not explicit but implicit; and the reader who does not grasp them artistically, but is merely looking for simple morals, is certain to be hopelessly confused. Especially will he be confused if the author *does* draw an explicit moral which is the opposite of or has nothing to do with his real purport. (278)

Also problematic, Wilson argued, was the tendency to disregard or devalue literary characters and conflicts that seemed socially unexceptional. A writer's "moral insight" was infinitely more important than the particulars of his literary situations.

Nor does it matter necessarily in a work of art whether the characters are shown engaged in a conflict which illustrates the larger conflicts of society or in one which from that point of view is trivial. In art. . . a sort of law of moral interchangeability prevails: we may transpose the actions and the sentiments that move us into terms of whatever we do or are ourselves. Real genius of moral insight is a motor which will start any engine. (278–79)

Finally, Wilson maintained, the effect of a literary work may not be contingent on the particular outcome of a story as a character. Once again, this was a simple-minded assumption of the inexperienced reader. "Nor does it necessarily matter, for the moral effect of a work of literature, whether the forces of bravery or virtue with which we identify ourselves are victorious or vanquished in the end" (279). In each of these areas, Wilson could have cited instances in which James Joyce's work had been unjustly attacked by cultural watchdogs of both the left and right.

Wilson's wide-ranging essay moved from an elaborate explanation and defense of Trotsky's cultural perspective, to indictments of Stalinist totalitarianism and repression, to a discussion of the intricacies of creating and interpreting "long-range" literature. It was futile, Wilson asserted, to try to create literature according to doctrine, as the advocates of socialist realism had attempted. Such an effort "always indicates sterility on the part of those who engage in it, and . . . always actually works, if it has any effect at all, to legislate good literature *out* of existence and to discourage the production of any more" (281). While great art may be a political weapon, it is not great or enduring art *because* it is so. Wilson's antipathy was not to Marxism but to Stalinism. Marxism, he argued, may not be useful in judging the quality of art, though it can illuminate its "origins and social significance." But the promise of Marxism, wrote Wilson, lay not in literary criticism but in political action. Paraphrasing Trotsky, Wilson suggested that under communism it was

society itself that became the work of art, the object
to be shaped and transformed. "In practicing and prizing
literature, we must not be unaware of the first efforts
of the human spirit to transcend literature itself" (289).

Wilson's groundbreaking essay on *Ulysses* in *Axel's Castle*
shows us a sophisticated critic wrestling with a complex
and revolutionary text, at once applauding its successes,
criticizing its failures, and puzzling over its intricacies and
ambiguities. Perhaps most importantly, Wilson tried in
earnest to understand *Ulysses* through its author's eyes.
Even when perplexed about some feature of the novel,
Wilson was willing to grant that Joyce may have had
some other purpose that would justify the scene or technique in question. And while Wilson perceived clearly the
revolutionary nature of *Ulysses*, he placed both text and
author inside a moral, intellectual, and artistic tradition
that made both seem less odd, less deviant, and less
obscure.

Wilson argued that Joyce exhibited both naturalist and
Symbolist tendencies in *Ulysses*, observing "all the Naturalistic restrictions in regard to the story [he] is telling at
the same time that [he] allows [himself] to exercise all the
Symbolistic privileges in regard to the way [he] tells it"
(207). Wilson especially admired Joyce's adaptation and
refinement of the naturalistic techniques of Flaubert: not
only did Joyce vividly recreate Dublin ("We possess Dublin, seen, heard, smelt and felt, brooded over, imagined,
remembered" [211]); he found "the unique vocabulary
and rhythm" to render its particular voices. In his penetrating exploration of the internal lives of his characters,
Joyce exploited Symbolist methods, but "Joyce's grasp

on his objective world never slips: his work is unshakably established on Naturalistic foundations" (204). Joyce, unlike Proust, avoided "falling over into [the] decadence of psychological fiction" (204). Wilson's diction was drawn from both the soapbox and the pulpit, but his perspective was more tolerant and more circumspect than that of the moralists or political ideologues.

It was the narrative of *Ulysses* that most engaged Wilson's interest, and although it was the interruption of that narrative with parodies and interpolations that caused him consternation, Wilson was not prepared to accept the contention of other critics that the novel was "too fluid or too chaotic." In fact, he wrote, "*Ulysses* suffers from an excess of design rather than from a lack of it" (211). With his many allusions and interpolations in the later episodes, Joyce "half burie[s] his story under the virtuosity of his technical devices" (215). "Sheer fantastic pedantry," Wilson called the interpolations in "Oxen of the Sun"; "artistically absolutely indefensible" (216). Wilson's impatience with Joyce's radical stylistic innovations echoed similar criticism from less enthusiastic reviewers of *Ulysses*. Wilson, however, differed in his ability to question his own assumptions and tastes. He concluded his chastisements by speculating that perhaps Joyce had purposes of his own that justified his choice of techniques: "perhaps . . . he did not, after all, quite want us to understand his story . . . [and] ended up throwing up between us and it a fortification of solemn burlesque prose" (217). Wilson humbly admitted at the end of the essay that "when we come to think about what we take at first to be the defects in Joyce's work, we find them so closely involved with the depth of his thought and the originality of his conception that we are obliged to grant them a certain necessity" (236).

Wilson, who in his eclectic reach would appropriate Freudian insights for his 1941 study, *The Wound and the Bow*, was fascinated by Joyce's "psychological portraiture," which he admired for its exhaustiveness and precision. Moreover, he was not offended by the unsentimentalized portrait of humankind that emerged from *Ulysses*. Joyce, he argued, did expose "the dirty, the trivial, and the base," but also explored more admirable human qualities: "love, nobility, truth, and virtue" (218). Joyce presented a balanced view of man, not, as some have argued, a misanthropic one. In fact, said Wilson, "Joyce is remarkable, rather, for equanimity"; "[he] exhibit[s] ordinary humanity without either satirizing it or sentimentalizing it" (220). Although Wilson's enthusiasms occasionally pushed him toward such overstatements as the latter, his thesis was sound. During an era in which anti-Semitism and elitism were not only unobjectionable but fashionable among the literary avant-garde, one of Joyce's distinctions as a modernist was his sympathetic portrayal of Bloom. Wilson refused to caricature Bloom or to lament that he was not a budding revolutionary or an antiseptic aristocrat. "[Bloom] is all the possibilities of that ordinary humanity which is somehow not so ordinary after all; and it is the proof of Joyce's greatness that, though we recognize Bloom's perfect truth and typical character, we cannot pigeonhole him in any familiar category, racial, social, moral, literary, or even. . . historical" (223).

While Wilson used the example of Bloom to refute the charge that Joyce was misanthropic, he implicitly used Molly to rebut allegations that Joyce was amoral or nihilistic. Molly, whom Wilson described as the "gross body, the body of humanity," redeemed herself in her choice of Bloom as husband and Stephen as fantasy lover and surrogate son. Wilson described her rejection of Boylan and acceptance of Bloom / Stephen as the "greatest moral climax of the story." "This gross body—upon which the whole structure of *Ulysses* rests—still throbbing with so strong a rhythm amid obscenity, commonness, and squalor—is laboring to throw up some knowledge and beauty by which it may transcend itself" (224). Wilson's moralizing may seem anachronistic, but his belief in the underlying moralism of the novel corresponds with more recent readings (for example, Richard Ellmann's in *The Consciousness of Joyce*) and seems an apt response to sanctimonious attacks on Joyce from more tendentious quarters. Wilson's Joyce affirmed reason over passion, knowledge and beauty over ignorance and strife. At the core of *Ulysses*, Wilson implied, were values which we recognize as progressive and enlightened.

At the same time, however, Wilson heralded Joyce as "the great poet of a new phase of the human consciousness" (221). Joyce captures the dynamism and vitality of urban life and the dissociation and relativism that mark the internal life of modern man. In *Ulysses*, and even more so in *Finnegans Wake*, wrote Wilson, Joyce takes us at least part of the way into a Proustian world of subjectivity and an Einsteinian world of relativity. In the universe of *Ulysses*, "everything is reduced to terms of 'events' like those of modern physics and philosophy—events which make up a 'continuum,' but which may be taken as infinitely small" (222). Moral values, social institutions, and personal identities emerge and recede, coalesce and dissolve. Wilson, who had earlier denounced the Humanists for clinging to an unrealistic, anachronistic conception of man, applauded Joyce's efforts to chronicle the changes in modern life and portray modern consciousness in its fullness and complexity.

Wilson viewed *Finnegans Wake*, "this immense poem of sleep" (*Wound and the Bow* 244) as a further step in the exploration of human consciousness and admired Joyce's experiment while expressing some of the same misgivings he had had about *Ulysses*. In "The Dream of H.C. Earwicker," written in 1939 and collected in *The Wound and the Bow*, Wilson explained and praised Joyce's ambitious project:

Finnegans Wake carries even further the kind of insight into such human relations which was already carried far in *Ulysses*; and it advances with an astounding stride the attempt to find the universally human in ordinary specialized experience which was implied in the earlier work by the Odyssean parallel. Joyce will now try to build up inductively the whole of human history and myth from the impulses, conscious and dormant, the unrealized potentialities, of a single human being, who is to be a man even more obscure and even less well-endowed, even less civilized and aspiring than was Bloom in *Ulysses*.

　Finnegans Wake, in conception as well as in execution, is one of the boldest books ever written. (254)

But it was the execution of the novel that Wilson found flawed, even more seriously than what he had viewed as the weaker sections of *Ulysses*. Wilson's objections were similar, though more severe. Earwicker's character becomes lost in the myriad of voices and myths attributed to him; "he is not so convincing as Bloom was: there has been too much literature poured into him" (259). Similarly, Earwicker's story becomes obscured and the novel loses dramatic power. Still suspended between a reverence for the old forms and a fascination with the new, Wilson complained about Joyce's "growing self-indulgence in an impulse to pure verbal play" (259).

I believe that the miscarriage of *Finnegans Wake*, in so far as it does miscarry, is due primarily to two tendencies of Joyce's which were already in evidence in *Ulysses*: the impulse, in the absence of dramatic power, to work up an epic impressiveness by multiplying and complicating detail, by filling in abstract diagrams and laying on intellectual conceits, till the organic at which he aims has been spoiled by too much that is synthetic; and a curious shrinking solicitude to conceal from the reader his real subjects. . . . The more daring Joyce's subjects become, the more he tends to swathe them about with the fancywork of his literary virtuosity. It is as if it were not merely Earwicker who was frightened by the state of his emotions but as if Joyce were embarrassed, too. (266–67)

Yet, having elaborated the novel's deficiencies, Wilson would in 1941 enter a long footnote at this juncture in his essay qualifying his criticisms and reaffirming the coherence and the mimetic power of all of Joyce's fiction. Here again, as in *Axel's Castle*, we witness Wilson intellectually stalking an enormously complicated work, assessing its strengths and weaknesses, arguing with himself continually over its meaning and importance.

I ought to amend what is said in this essay on the basis of a first reading by adding that *Finnegans Wake*, like *Ulysses*, gets better the more you go back to it. I do not know of any other books of which it is true as it is of Joyce's. . . . That this should be true is due probably to some special defect of rapport between Joyce and the audience he is addressing, to some disease of his architectural faculty; but he compensates us partly for this by giving us more in the long run than we had realized at first was there and he eventually produces the illusion that his fiction has a reality like life's, because, behind all the antics, the pedantry, the artificial patterns, something organic and independent of these is always revealing itself; and we end by recomposing a world in our mind as we do from the phenomena of experience. (266)

Wilson's general enthusiasm for Joyce's work was not always shared by others on the left who migrated toward the Trotskyist cultural perspective. Philip Rahv, one of the central figures in the cultural warfare of the thirties, did not embrace Joyce's work, though philosophically his views were in consonance with Wilson's and Farrell's. Along with many others, Rahv changed his theoretical positions during the decade. Two of his most influential essays, "Problems and Perspectives in Proletarian Literature" and "Proletarian Literature: A Political Autopsy" (1934 and 1939 respectively), reflect his initial, qualified acceptance of the movement toward proletarian literature and his later disenchantment with that movement and its sponsors. In the editorial pages of *Partisan Review*, Rahv emerged as one of the principal spokesmen for the dissident left. In a retrospective essay written in 1967, he described this group: "Though by no means 'orthodox' in our approach to Marxism, we did not think of ourselves as abandoning its basic program and ideals; least of all did we think ourselves as errant sons returning to the 'bourgeois' fold" (*Essays* 341).

Rahv's 1934 essay, coauthored with William Phillips ("Wallace Phelps"), endorsed the idea of a revolutionary literature ("the bone and flesh of revolutionary sensibility taking on literary form" [53]) but cautioned against the literary abuses of what the authors disparagingly referred to as "leftism." The new literature offered the possibility of "a new way of looking at life" and a new "solidarity" with one's reader. The authors criticized the "aesthetes of

the twenties" for their elitism, their skepticism, and their
passivity. But they also warned that revolutionary literature may be vulgarized by the intrusion of Communist
party doctrine.

"Leftism," by tacking on political perspectives to awkward
literary forms, drains literature of its more specific qualities.
Unacquainted with the real experiences of workers, "leftism"
in criticism and creation alike, hides behind a smoke-screen of
verbal revolutionism. It assumes a direct line between economic base and ideology, and in this way distorts and vulgar-
izes the complexity of human nature, the motives of action
and their expression in thought and feeling. ("Problems" 5)

Rahv and Phillips called for a new kind of literature, one
more accessible and more sympathetic to the struggles of
working people, but they insisted that the new literature
be literature, not ideology. At the same time, they
announced that they would not tolerate the "right wing
tendency," which inclined toward "political fence-
straddling"; writers guilty of this offense must be given
"concrete direction in order to. . . overcome their backward views as quickly as possible" (6). They themselves
thus endorsed the kind of ideological conformity that
they disparaged among "leftists." Their oscillations in
this essay between aesthetic and political allegiances indicated their own uncertainty over just what role politics
ought to play in the new literature they proposed.
    In an essay published later in the same year, entitled
"How the Wasteland Became a Flower Garden," Rahv
took issue with the views of Joseph Wood Krutch, who
had belittled Marxism and criticized its influence on literature. Krutch turned the artist into a counterrevolutionary, argued Rahv; his "bourgeois literature" encouraged
complacency and ultimately invited the spread of fascism.

Rahv called for a revolutionary literature, one that "embodies the struggle of the producing masses against their plunderers" (39). Bourgeois literature, "by no means homogenous," may be a "stimulus to social insurgence" or may insulate readers from such activity. Rahv believed that most bourgeois literature, including Joyce's work, failed as effective social protest because it did not identify and challenge the "predatory social order" that was at the root of social problems. Instead, it ended up idealizing its own negations and becoming obsessed with aesthetic theory. It did not lead its readers to heightened class consciousness. Rahv cited Joyce as an example:

From the initial social resentment in *Dubliners* Joyce developed toward a demoralized consciousness of social impotence and hence toward a desire for liberation from the social. The result is a sinking into imaginative life, regarded as the self-contained domain of art: thus art becomes a barrier between his disgust with reality and his impulse to change it. The perfect stasis is the idealized negation, which other writers paralleled with similar dogmas of passivity. (42)

Rahv dismissed Joyce's later work, especially *Finnegans Wake*, as solipsistic and finally counterrevolutionary. His reading of Joyce thus echoed commentary by Cowley, Eastman, and even Mirsky and Radek. At this point in his career, Rahv applied strict political criteria to his evaluation of Joyce, and found him wanting.

Rahv gave us further evidence of his distaste for Joyce in a review of Stephen Spender's *The Destructive Element* in *Partisan Review* in 1936. Rahv referred to Spender's analysis of Joyce as "the best on the subject": "His insight into the weaknesses of Joyce, which the gravity and size

of *Ulysses* have tended to obscure for most critics, is of
extreme value for a definition of what Joyce did achieve"
("Aesthetic of Migration" 29). Spender, who, for a brief
time in 1936 and 1937 would become a member of the
British Communist Party, gave *Ulysses* an ambivalent but
generally unfavorable review. He seemed genuinely confused by the novel and contradicted himself repeatedly in
his essay. He described the novel as on the verge of
chaos, then later declared that it "is complete, with no
loose ends" (86). *Ulysses* "leaves in the mouth the taste of
dust and ashes, although the most persistent note of the
book is one of geniality" (84). Bloom is "magnificent,"
yet he is a "compact little Jew, whose brain crawls with
undeveloped romantic and scientific ideas, like larvae of
insects" (80). Spender was less equivocal about the elements of the novel that disturbed him: Joyce's style and
content were monotonous; his "factual realism" was too
strong; he remained too detached, too unemotional; his
revelations of the workings of the unconscious mind were
tasteless and offensive. Spender closed his commentary
with some rather odd moralizing that is reminiscent of
remarks made by Paul Elmer More about *Ulysses*: "It is
this physical obsession [with the wickedness of the body]
which permeates *Ulysses*. Sin and death are all that is
left of the Church even. There is no belief in salvation . . . only a nightmare vision of a world smelling with
the dregs of a hated Catholicism, endless sin and no
salvation" (86). We are left to wonder what it was that
Rahv so admired in Spender's review. Perhaps Rahv saw
a political import in Spender's religious analysis: the
"other" salvation that *Ulysses* does not offer is the likeli-
hood of a proletarian revolution. Such an interpretation is
not farfetched. Rahv himself would later describe the decade of the 1930s as one of "ideological vulgarity and

opportunism, of double-think and power-worship, maintained throughout by a mean and crude and unthinking kind of secular religiosity" (*Essays* 336).

Rahv would repudiate proletarian literature and soften his views considerably toward "bourgeois" literature later in the thirties. His changes were most apparent in "Proletarian Literature: A Political Autopsy," which appeared in the *Southern Review* in 1939. There he branded proletarian literature "the literature of a party disguised as the literature of a class." What resulted were crude, schematized novels; the creativity of the left was "stuff[ed] . . . into the sack of political orthodoxy" (299–300). Rahv angrily asserted that the movement for proletarian literature was "an episode in the history of totalitarian communism" which "will be remembered as a comedy of mistaken identities and the tragedy of a frustrated social impulse in contemporary letters" (296).

Rahv went further in his indictment of this movement, insisting that it was a mistake to assume the working class could produce its own literature. Those who create and perpetuate culture emerge from the ruling classes.

Literature is the outgrowth of a whole culture. . . . A class which has no culture of its own can have no literature either. Now in all class societies it is the ruling class alone which possesses both the material means and the self-consciousness . . . that are the prerequisites of cultural creation. As an oppressed class, the proletariat, insofar as it is a cultural consumer, lives on the leavings of the bourgeoisie. It has neither the means nor the consciousness necessary for cultural self-differentiation. (304)

Rahv had clearly adopted a new perspective toward what he had disdainfully referred to as "bourgeois literature" in his earlier essays. He appeared much more sympathetic to the dilemmas of the bourgeois artist, at times even defending him against his own earlier criticism. "The modern artist has been rebuked time and again by social-minded critics both of the Right and of the Left for his obsessive introversion, his jealously maintained privacy, his aesthetic mysticism, his bent toward the obscure and the morbid. Yet without such qualities, given the boundaries of the bourgeois world, he could not have survived" (297–98). In contrast to the shallowness of proletarian art, Rahv suggested that the "older tradition" was "more 'progressive'. . . more disinterested, [and] infinitely more sensitive to the actual conditions of human existence" (306).

Rahv leaves us to speculate on what his revised opinion of Joyce might have been. But given the shifts in his political and aesthetic perspectives so apparent in his essays from the late thirties, we might fairly assume that Joyce had risen in his estimation. When in 1939 Rahv warned the artist not to deceive himself with "bureaucratized visions of the shining cities of the future" but instead to be "faithful to the metamorphosis of the present" (309), we can see that he had moved closer philosophically to Trotsky, Farrell, and Wilson. And we might reasonably argue that, from this new perspective, he showed at least a tacit acceptance of Joyce's work and sensibility.

Rahv's engagement with Joyce's work was incidental, clearly subordinate to his interest in defining the relationship between Marxist theory and literary practice. The magazine which he edited, *Partisan Review*, had from its inception sought to bring together revolutionary tem-

peraments in both politics and art. Having suspended its
publication in 1936, Rahv and coeditor William Phillips
brought out a reorganized *Partisan Review* in 1937. The
new publication would be militantly anti-Stalinist and
zealously committed to modernist literature. As Rahv
and others had learned from their experiences earlier in
the decade, alliances between political and artistic interests were fraught with danger. No one among those
associated with Trotskyism viewed such alliances more
suspiciously than Lionel Trilling.

In marked contrast to Rahv's, Trilling's work during
the 1930s and early 1940s seems curiously detached
from the political and cultural imbroglios of the time.
Although he was repulsed by the vulgar excesses of proletarian literature, and though his sympathies were clearly
with the Trotskyists, Trilling pursued interests and
opinions that were more purely literary. His effort was
unmistakably to subordinate politics to literature in the
hope of obtaining a larger understanding of both. In the
words of William M. Chace, Trilling insisted on

recognizing the full implications of politics while being always
mindful of its secondary status. . . . Reading Trilling, one is
always aware of that complexity: he is of the American 1930s
and of the generation of New York thinkers profoundly shaped
by that decade's turmoil, yet he stands oddly aside from those
times, and from his colleagues and their intensities. (*Lionel
Trilling* 18)

One of Trilling's earliest published comments on Joyce
appeared in his 1940 essay, "Freud and Literature." Like
Edmund Wilson before him, Trilling was fascinated by
Joyce's psychological explorations and pointed out
Joyce's indebtedness to Freud: "James Joyce, with his in-

terest in the numerous states of receding consciousness, with his use of words as things and of words which point to more than one thing, with his pervading sense of the interrelation and interpenetration of all things, and, not least important, his treatment of familial themes, has perhaps most thoroughly and consciously exploited Freud's ideas" (40).

Trilling's most extensive comments on Joyce appeared in a 1968 essay ("James Joyce in His Letters") marking the publication of two new volumes of Joyce's letters. Not surprisingly, Trilling's reading of Joyce touched on few of the controversies from the 1930s. It was instead a penetrating, finely nuanced study of Joyce's vision and sensibility, one which reached unusually gloomy conclusions. Although Trilling demonstrated a much more discerning eye than the conservatives of the thirties, and though he wrote with none of their polemical fervor, his conclusions about the underlying nihilism in Joyce's work sound oddly similar to their own. Trilling, however, seemed willing to celebrate Joyce's vision, or at least to congratulate him for his courage.

Trilling framed his essay around several lines excerpted from one of Joyce's letters to his son: "Here I conclude. My eyes are tired. For over half a century they have gazed into nullity, where they have found a lovely nothing." Trilling was intrigued by the oxymoronic "lovely nothing." He argued that "the power of Joyce's work derives . . . not only from the impulse to resist nullity but also, and equally, from the impulse to make nullity prevail" (144). Trilling took issue with the tendency (originating, no doubt, with Edmund Wilson's commentary on Joyce) to regard Joyce as a "positive" writer who warded off "nullity" through his creative acts. This was only partly true, argued Trilling. Joyce did conclude

Ulysses with Molly's life-affirming "yes," and he "con-
trived a rich poetry out of the humble and sordid, the
sad repeated round of the commonplace, laying a significant emphasis on the little, nameless, unremembered
acts of kindness and of love" (144). But Joyce was a "partisan" of that nullity, that entropic desire, that "paralysis
of the will" that pervaded *Dubliners*. Perhaps Joyce was
saying in his letter that "human existence is nullity right
enough, yet if it is looked into with a vision such as his,
the nothing that can be perceived really is lovely, though
the maintenance of that vision really is fatiguing work"
(143).

William M. Chace suggests that this portrait of Joyce
as one who painstakingly struggled toward nihilism corresponded with Trilling's own temperament and critical
practice.

Trilling is sustained in the late 1960s as Joyce was once sustained, by the capacity he has to measure the world fully and
carefully, never to divine its secrets too quickly, never to come
upon its truths prematurely. Joyce allows himself the fullest
amplitude in entertaining the complexities of the world; then he
finds the world vacuous. His genius rests on a kind of exalted
patience. Trilling's craft as a critic does likewise. (*Lionel Trilling*
143)

Trilling had discovered a Joyce who was his *semblable*.
Trilling's Joyce, like Trilling himself, was moving away
from engagement with the "merely human" and toward
some transcendent apprehension of the futility and the
illusory nature of existence. Such a reading of Joyce,
Chace adds, is incomplete. Joyce's work and Joyce's
thinking did not stop with the recognition of that "lovely
nothing" at the center of life. The Joycean dialectic never

forsook the human dimension; "Ithaca" would be succeeded by "Penelope." Trilling, however, "heard only
the doleful Joycean music" (*Lionel Trilling* 145).

With the exception of some involvement early in the
decade, Trilling was not actively engaged in the political
turmoil of the thirties. Nevertheless, his sensibility could
not help but be affected by it. In *The Liberal Imagination*
(1950) both his exhortations to intellectuals to restore "a
sense of variousness and possibility" to culture and his
definition of literature as "the human activity that takes
the fullest and most precise account of variousness, possibility, complexity, and difficulty" (xii) indicate his aversion
to the straitjacketing of cultural life that characterized the
thirties. He valued literature not for its ideology, but for
its ideas. The power of truly great literature, he declared,
was not to confirm our prejudices, but to "absorb and
disturb us in secret ways" (*Liberal Imagination* 283). In unraveling at least some of the complexity of *Ulysses*, Trilling did, indeed, document the novel's power to disturb.

Trilling was not the only reader of Joyce to conclude that
Joyce found nothing lovely at the center of existence.
Such a conclusion, of course, had serious cultural and
political implications, particularly in the 1930s, when *no*
conclusion seemed to lack such implications. Critics from
both political extremes protested either Joyce's utter lack
of affirmation or his tentative and oblique manner of declaring what affirmations he made.

As we have seen, Edmund Wilson and others defended
Joyce against the charge that his writing was nihilistic and
presented a portrait of an artist who quietly espoused
liberal and progressive values. Dwight Macdonald, for

example, referred to *Ulysses* as "a work overflowing with genial delight in the richness of human life"; he conceded that Joyce "rejected. . . a specific historical and social order," but only by so doing was he "able to survive as an artist and. . . preserve and defend those general human values on which culture depends" (449). Jeremy Hawthorn, in a recent summary and critique of Marxist commentary on *Ulysses*, asserts that there is a "value-centre" in the novel "that allows Joyce to make [it] such an affirmation of human values." He complains that most Marxists ignore the novel's humor, which, he argues, confirms certain "shared values" and "common perceptions" (123).

It is inaccurate to conclude that because Joyce was cynical about the uses to which culture could be put, he was a cultural cynic or nihilist. Joyce's art did not serve particular political or social ends, nor did it satisfy those critics who insisted that all art should do so. But although Joyce's work abounds in references to politics, and although Joyce himself had held strong political opinions early in his career, his fiction endorsed no political position nor espoused any political doctrine. But neither did it avoid the social and political issues that pressed themselves upon the consciousness of the Irish whom Joyce so faithfully recreated in his fiction. Joyce considered political disengagement to be vital to his creative freedom. As an artist, he viewed ideological conformity as anathema to his creative endeavors. He found a congenial audience among Farrell, Wilson, and others who insisted that his work be judged according to aesthetic rather than political criteria.

There were, of course, many factors which drew critics to Joyce's defense in the 1930s and afterwards. In addition to his technical virtuosity, Joyce's liberal sensibility and

espousal of essentially progressive values won him favor
from like-minded critics—critics who defended him the
more ardently from the crassness, the extremism, and the
intolerance demonstrated by ideologues from the right
and the left. Joyce, like Wilson, Trilling, and Farrell,
moved against the illiberal spirit of his time. He eschewed
tragic and heroic themes and celebrated what Irving
Howe has called the "public virtues" of liberalism:
"doubt, hesitation, and irony." We close with Howe's
appreciation of *Ulysses*:

If we glance at the greatest work of fiction composed in
English during our century, we find at its center a roly-poly
pacific Jew, a small figure of tolerance, muddle, and affection, a
figure quite the opposite of the hero, a man liberal almost by
default, as if he could not be anything else. Yet in these comic
limitations there are values to be honored, a precious sediment
of civilization. ("Literature and Liberalism" xxiii)

4

"On the Side of the Angels": Joyce and the New Critics

Joyce is a literary giant, an object of universal attention, and I think a critic is not censorious in remarking with concern the role he has assumed on so prodigious a scale. . . . Yet Joyce's book [*Finnegans Wake*] is on the side of the angels, and I do not like to abuse it.

JOHN CROWE RANSOM, 1939

If the politicians had been able to read Proust, or Joyce, or even Kafka, might they not have discerned more sharply what the trouble was and done something to avert the collapse? I doubt it; but it makes as much sense as the argument that literature can be a cause of social decay.

ALLEN TATE, 1951

[*Ulysses*] is not pure expressionism, or incomplete or impure expressionism; it is a rational and traditional art. To exaggerate only a little by repetition, *Ulysses* is the most structured book in English since at least Milton and it does as much to maintain and develop the full language as anybody since Shakespeare.   R. P. BLACKMUR, 1956

Among the medley of voices that clamored for cultural authority in America during the 1930s, a chorus of disenchanted Southerners arose in opposition to the countervailing appeals of the New Humanists and Communists. Distressed by the advance of Northern industrialism, deeply disturbed by the encroachment of politics and religion upon the arts, the Southern Agrarians wedded a reactionary social vision to a radical aesthetic theory and spawned a critical movement that would shift the emphases of literary criticism for years to come. Their manifesto, published in 1930 under the title *I'll Take My Stand*, was a rebuke to the cultural claims of the left and right as well as a plea for the revival of a way of life mythically embodied in the old South.

It is hardly surprising that, given the impracticality and vagueness of their social schemes, the Southern Agrarians are best known for their aesthetic formulations and better remembered as the New Critics. The most noteworthy among this group—John Crowe Ransom, Allen Tate, Robert Penn Warren, and Cleanth Brooks—would either abandon their agrarian program or softpeddle it as they became more wholly absorbed in the delineation of aesthetic theory in the late thirties and early forties. Ransom, Tate, and Warren had begun their careers with more purely literary ambitions, editing the periodical *The Fugitives* in the twenties. Their contributions to *I'll Take My Stand* marked the peak of their involvement in the ongoing debate over American social policy during the thirties.

Nevertheless, their social and political views are noteworthy, not least because they were often at odds with their aesthetic values. While the Agrarians held a crudely reactionary social perspective, they were in the vanguard of literary change. They applauded modernist formal innovations while yearning for the return of the "squirearchy" of the old South.[1] They developed a complex and finely nuanced critical method while lambasting the evils of industrialism, urbanization, and black emancipation. Although the configuration of their utopic society had a particular regional flavor and design, they shared with Ezra Pound and T. S. Eliot common grievances and ideals. In substance, the Agrarians envisioned a social arrangement that would allow an elite culture to flourish; that would award artistic creation before material production; that would confer dignity upon leisure activities before labor. Like Pound, Eliot, and Wyndham Lewis, the Agrarians were engaged in a quarrel with the modern world, and they looked backward for a model of social decorum they could invoke as an alternative to the chaos and dehumanization of contemporary life. They took refuge in the realm of aesthetics, where the possibility of perfect form was a reprieve from the fractured, alienated experience of modern man.

What did Agrarianism consist of? What was the substance of the Agrarians' vision? They believed that man was a fallen creature, finally imperfectible, despite what progressives and social scientists so loudly proclaimed. They disputed the idealism of liberals and radicals and rejected the notion that art ought to be a tool for moral and social reform. Art could be a satisfying sublimation, "transform[ing] instinctive experience into esthetic experience" (Kazin, *Native Grounds* 434), and could effectively illuminate our condition, but it could not remake man or save him from his own "precarious" condition (Ransom, "Reconstructed" 4). Such notions were the fallacies of a society ruled by science and unfettered reason.

The Agrarians insisted that the proper vocation for man was farming ("The world [must be] made safe for the farmers" was Ransom's paraphrase of Woodrow Wilson ["Reconstructed" 25]) and that science had given man a false sense of superiority over the land and over nature. They yearned for a restoration of the rural South, which, as Alfred Kazin noted, they mythologized as ardently as American Communists idealized Mother Russia. Theirs was the genteel South, prosperous for the privileged few, resplendent in the "amenities of life": "manners, conversation, hospitality, sympathy, family life, romantic love" (Davidson et al. xxv). Ransom invoked this sentimentalized image of the old South in his essay, "Reconstructed but Unregenerate," in *I'll Take My Stand*: "It was a kindly society, yet a realistic one; for it was a failure if it could not be said that people were for the most part in their right places. Slavery was a feature monstrous enough in theory, but, more often than not, humane in practice; and it is impossible to believe that its abolition alone could have effected any great revolution in society" (14). The Agrarians indulged themselves unabashedly in their own nostalgia, constructing from their wishes more than their memories a world of tranquility and order. They conceded the impracticality of their utopic visions in contemporary life. In their "Statement of Principles" at the beginning of *I'll Take My Stand*, they confessed,

"These principles do not intend to be very specific in proposing any practical measures" (Davidson et al. xxix).

Aesthetic questions became the major preoccupation of the Agrarians during the 1930s, and despite its appearance to the contrary, the aesthetic they embraced was a response to and an evocation of political ideals. It was first a reaction to the injection of politics and religion into aesthetic debate by moralists of the left and the right, by Stalinists and New Humanists. Ransom, in an essay entitled "Criticism, Inc." (1938), chastised both groups for being "diversionists": "It is just as proper for [the proletarians] . . . to make literature serve the cause of loving-comradeship, as it is for the Humanists to censure romanticism. . . These procedures are of the same sort" (457). Criticism, Ransom argued, was a difficult, highly specialized occupation, best reserved for trained academicians. "[I]t is not anybody who can do criticism," he intoned (457).

In their insistence that criticism be solely occupied with aesthetic matters, the New Critics fetishized literary form and turned criticism into a more taxing, more cerebral, and more professional activity. They probed the intricacies, the tensions, and the mysteries of literary form with the fervor of religious pilgrims and the fastidiousness of laboratory scientists. They practiced, ironically enough, a peculiar form of decadence, according to Alfred Kazin, one which "specialized in isolated ecstasies. . . cut off from the main sources of life and floundering in the sick self-justification of aestheticism."

Form had. . . become a sentimental symbol of order in a world that had no order. . . . At bottom their form was always an indeterminate vision of some secret ideal, an ideal fundamentally vague and incommunicable, and therefore in the service of every personal association of snobbery, eccentricity, rigidity, malice, or plain ignorance the critic might reveal. (*Native Grounds* 431)

In their effort to free criticism of the influence of politics and ethics, the New Critics developed an aesthetic with self-serving political implications of its own. They laid the groundwork for a cultural aristocracy governed by the master exegetes of form, the "dour professional[s]" (Kazin 432) of Criticism, Inc.

The effect of the New Criticism was to decontextualize literature, to isolate it outside the social fabric and ignore its political import. Its practitioners were as compulsive in their attention to form as in their disregard of a writer's political views. They viewed a writer's responsibility to be entirely to his conscience and to his craft. In "To Whom Is the Poet Responsible?" (1951) Allen Tate criticized Ezra Pound and Archibald MacLeish for their political activities and confessed:

[T]he political responsibility of poets bores me. . . . It irritates me because the poet has a great responsibility of his own: it is the responsibility to be a poet, to write poems, and not to gad about using the rumor of his verse . . . as the excuse to appear on platforms. . . . I have a deep, unbecoming suspicion of such talking poets: whatever other desirable things they may believe in, they do not believe in poetry. (26)

Tate, however, would not dismiss Pound's work because of his politics. He found Pound's dedication to his verse sufficient, and could overlook his "childish and detestable" political opinions in voting to award him the Bollingen Prize for Poetry in 1949. As he explained, "The specific task of the man of letters is to attend to the health of society not at large but through literature—that is, he must be constantly aware of the condition of language in his age. . . . [Pound] had done more than any other man to regenerate the language, if not the imaginative forms, of English verse" ("Ezra Pound" 511). How strikingly different was this definition of a writer's responsibility from Van Wyck Brooks's exhortations, offered only a decade earlier, to artists to be "voices of the people."

Although Tate felt it appropriate to reward Pound's poetry, the New Critical response to modernism was not without reservation or ambivalence. Since the New Critics were concerned primarily with poetry, they addressed themselves most frequently to the work of Pound and Eliot. While they were distressed by Pound's political fanaticism and worried over Eliot's religious orthodoxy, they were relieved to find their poetry relatively free of these encumbrances. Eliot's achievement, said Ransom, was "his habit of considering aesthetic effect as independent of religious effect, or moral, or political and social; as an end that is beyond and is not coordinate with these" ("T. S. Eliot" 138). Though the New Critics were themselves religiously orthodox and politically conservative, these interests were not to dictate the subjects of their own poetry.

While they attended almost exclusively to the formal qualities of modernist literature, and found much to admire, Tate and Ransom and others found it more difficult to accept elements of the modernist temperament. They shared Eliot and Pound's contempt for the modern world, but they could not embrace the cynicism and nihilism that they generally associated with modernism. They were troubled by the aggressively antitraditionalist posture of the modernists, since in the early thirties they were earnestly struggling to salvage a social and cultural tradition from their own past. "[T]he South has always been slow to question the authority of habit," wrote Ransom in 1935. "It is not here you will find your revolutions" ("Modern" 185). Southerners ought to regard modernism warily, he advised.

The substance of modernism is not a technique but an attitude. And a dangerous attitude. . . . Modernism is a progressive disease, and we in the Occident are in an advanced stage of it, says Mr. Krutch. . . . Modernism is skepticism and disillusionment, and ends in despair. We come to such a degree of self-consciousness that we question our natural motives of action and our inherited patterns of behavior. . . . Thus we commit a spiritual suicide. ("Modern" 184–85)

Ransom was more suspicious of modernism than Tate, particularly of its influence on Southern writers. "I cannot assume," Tate wrote in 1935, "as Mr. Ransom seems to do, that exposure to the world of modernism . . . was of itself a demoralizing experience" ("*Profession*" 531–32). In 1941 and 1942, when Van Wyck Brooks delivered a vitriolic attack on Joyce and other modernists and Dwight Macdonald responded with an impassioned defense in *Partisan Review*, Tate sided with Macdonald, Ransom with Brooks.[2] Tate equated Brooks's diatribe with the Nazis' attack on modern art. "Brooks," he maintained, "holds the moralistic and didactic view which can be extended, as he has extended it, into the nationalist and patriotic view. And this view can believe in the dignity of man only by sticking its head in the sand" ("Brooks-MacLeish" 38). Ransom, on the other hand, agreed with Brooks's thesis that "our literature with its brilliance is less creative and positive than other literatures have been." He railed not only against "tractarian" and "mass-produced literature," but also against "the fiction so 'pure' that it is richly detailed to the point of being without direction, and fantastic and obscure" ("Brooks-MacLeish" 40).

To a critic of Tate's temperament, it was clearly not the obscurity or complexity of the modernist canon that gave pause. One of Pound's cantos or Eliot's poems taxed all of the critic's exegetical skills, justifying Ransom's call for the professionalization of the trade. Tate, too, deplored the lack of sophisticated readers. In two essays that appeared in 1935, "Tension in Poetry" and "Understanding Modern Poetry," Tate disputed Max Eastman's claim that modern poets were "unintelligible"; rather, Tate protested, modern readers were unintelligent: "poetry [has] become a very difficult affair, demanding both in its writing and in its reading all the intellectual power that we have" (*Reason* 84). It was fallacious to assume, as Eastman had, that poetry consisted of simple "communication." "The meaning of poetry is its 'tension,' the full organized body of all the extension and intension that we can find in it" (*Reason* 72). Eastman, Tate maintained, had assumed the role of debater and scientist rather than critic; he was too self-assuredly searching for "truths" in poetry rather than allowing for the existence of mystery and ambiguity.

Indeed, it was preeminently this quest—this search for the "tensions," the nuances, the unresolvable elements of the text—that engaged the New Critics. Literature, Tate insisted, ought not to be written or read as a political tract or scientific treatise. Its meaning was more abstruse, less resolved, and finally ineffable. The finest literature, like the best poets, did not "talk" but whispered, in mysterious language, to smaller and more refined audiences, to the "few choicer spirits" whom Ransom pre-

dicted would inherit the mantle of criticism (quoted in
Young xix). When the New Critic considered a modernist
text, he was engaged by its craft and complexity, its subtleties and ironies, its vagaries and contradictions. And in
Joyce's work it was invariably these elements that he
emphasized and explored.

Had Joyce written more poetry than fiction, he would
have received more attention from the New Critics and
perhaps earned more praise than his contemporaries
Pound and Eliot. Joyce appeared to fit more perfectly the
artistic mold set by the New Critics: a recluse, wholly devoted to his craft, immersed in the permutations and
complexities of language. Moreover, Joyce was unen-
cumbered by Eliot's religious orthodoxy or Pound's
political fanaticism; he was not a "talking" poet. Still,
there was a troubling political and social content in
Joyce's work that the New Critics could not wholly
ignore. Despite Joyce's technical virtuosity, there was
wandering through *Ulysses* an unrefined, middle-class
Jew named Bloom; there was Dublin itself, surging with
activity and corruption; there were the debased figures
of the modern artist, Stephen Dedalus, and the unrepentant adultress, Molly Bloom. Vestiges of high culture in
Ulysses were mocked or displaced by artifacts of low
culture; political and religious authorities were ridiculed;
aesthetic theory was finally revealed to be sham and
pretense. Had Tate and Ransom subjected *Ulysses* to close
reading—and no evidence suggests that they did—they
could hardly have neglected these disquieting elements of
the novel.

    Of those most closely associated with New Criticism—Tate, Ransom, Warren, and Brooks—only Cleanth Brooks published on *Ulysses*. Tate contributed an analysis of "The Dead" in his anthology, *The House of Fiction* (1950), while Ransom devoted an essay to *Finnegans Wake* in the *Kenyon Review* (1939). But only Brooks gave *Ulysses* any close consideration, and then not until 1968. R. P. Blackmur, whose critical perspective was influenced by the work of the New Critics, also examined *Ulysses* in some detail in essays published in the forties and fifties.

Before considering Brooks's and Blackmur's comments on *Ulysses*, let us look briefly at Tate's remarks on "The Dead." In his close reading Tate focused on the story's technical sophistication. He examined Joyce's use of the "Roving Narrator," which, apropos of the times, he renamed the "Central Intelligence" in his revised commentary for the 1960 second edition of *The House of Fiction*. Joyce's narrative technique allowed the reader to be simultaneously inside and outside the characters, to be dramatically engaged while still able to view them with ironic detachment. He applauded Joyce's use of naturalistic detail, which was all the more effective because it operated on a symbolic as well as a dramatic level. Echoing to some degree Edmund Wilson's praise of *Ulysses*, Tate remarked that Joyce deftly exploited both naturalistic and Symbolistic techniques. The central symbol of "The Dead," Tate noted, was the snow, which reversed its meaning in the course of the story. While at the beginning it represented a cold, external force and suggested Gabriel Conroy's indifference to humankind, at story's end it became a symbol of warmth and expanded consciousness: "It stands for Gabriel's escape from his own ego into the larger world of humanity, including 'all the living and the dead'" (*House of Fiction* 186). Tate concurred with T. S. Eliot's conclusion about this story: so emblematic of Joyce's work, it was "penetrated with Christian feeling."

Tate's attention to the details and structure of "The Dead" was similar to the emphasis given by Cleanth Brooks in his analyses of "Clay" and *Ulysses*. Brooks admired "Clay" as a "richly and delicately organized" work. "Its verbal texture resembles so nearly to the density of lyric poetry that the reading that it requires is more intense than that which is adequate for the style of fictional prose" (52). Joyce's prose was appealing precisely because it resembled verse in its compactness, its precise modulation, and its associative power. Brooks's essay on *Ulysses* reflected this same appreciation for Joyce's poetic gifts. His title, "Joyce's *Ulysses*: Symbolic Poem, Biography, or Novel?" implied his grateful acknowledgment that *Ulysses* was, indeed, a different kind of novel.

Brooks began his essay by taking up the argument over whether *Ulysses* was a "ragbag" of the author's memories or a well-crafted novel. Citing R. M. Adams's study, *Surface and Symbol: The Consistency of James Joyce's "Ulysses"*, Brooks argued that there was more coherence in *Ulysses* than Adams granted. Upon close analysis, the apparently functionless elements in the novel—what Adams identified as "surface" more than "symbol"—did have an integral place in the narrative. Brooks detected subtler patterns in the novel than Adams had noticed. *Ulysses* could be categorized as a novel because it presented a coherent pattern of symbols that yielded a coherent system of values or meanings. Brooks was particularly pleased with the novel's opening chapters, which he described as "a brilliant dramatization of. . . the alienation of the sensitive artist in our day" (81). Brooks disputed claims that *Ulysses* was too esoteric or too inaccessible: "It is a novel, and yields, in spite of its special difficulties, the sort of knowledge about ourselves and about our world that any other authentic novel does yield" (86).

What was the knowledge that *Ulysses* offered? Brooks argued that the novel explored the "rift in modern civilization" (86) which was embodied in its three major characters: the "sensitive artist," the "bumbling bourgeois," and the "nature female." *Ulysses* was, in microcosm, a portrait of a fragmented, conflict-ridden society. The novel's most significant moments were those in which contraries collided, when Bloom and Stephen, then Bloom and Molly came together and offered the potential of union or reconciliation. But Brooks cautioned against reading the novel sentimentally; the evidence from the text did not support the notion that either a union or a reconciliation had occurred.

Commentators, in their anxiety to find a happy ending, have insisted on the book's compassion and on its final optimism, and have oversimplified and distorted its meaning. In any case, whatever conclusions about the meaning of the novel we are to draw will require testing against the fictional structure—will have to be matched with what can actually be found in the novel. (86)

Brooks, noting the details of the text with scientific acumen, insisted on preserving its tensions, its ambiguities, and its paradoxes. "There is a great deal of comedy in *Ulysses*, though it does not bar out pathos" (86).

Brooks's close and sensitive reading of *Ulysses* was noteworthy for its appreciation of the novel's depth and intricate structure. He admitted *Ulysses* into the novelistic canon, though to do so in 1968 was less than a bold stroke. Brooks, like such other sympathetic readers of *Ulysses* as Edmund Wilson, was a patient and admiring student of the novel. He scoured it for evidence to refute superficial or simple-minded readings. He applied the same careful scrutiny and revealed the same fondness for textual ambiguity that Tate and Ransom had in their considerations of poetry. Interesting too was Brooks's sympathetic response to hapless Stephen Dedalus, whom few readers have found so likable. Undoubtedly, there was some identification between Brooks, whose early allegiance had been to another group of literary exiles, the Southern Agrarians, and the alienated and besieged artist figure, Stephen Dedalus. And while Brooks's interpretation of *Ulysses* drew convincingly on evidence from the novel, there seems a degree of critical will or wish in his insistence that no communion had occurred between Stephen and that "bumbling, bourgeois citizen," dilletantish Leopold Bloom. Stephen's isolation and artistic integrity were not thereby compromised; he assumed a tragic rather than a comic posture. And he would continue to epitomize the image of the modern artist conceived by the Agrarians—the image they beheld most vividly in their own reflections.

John Crowe Ransom's essay, "The Aesthetics of *Finnegans Wake*," which appeared in the *Kenyon Review* in 1939, was in part an appreciation of the book, in part an appropriation of it. Faulting the book's apologists and detractors for being too "uncritical," Ransom presumptively declared the *Wake* to be both a failure and a success. While there was no "close logic" to the book and its parts, and while Joyce "obfuscate[d] discourse" by the use of puns and the stream-of-consciousness technique, the *Wake* challenged reigning epistemology and represented something of a model and inspiration for poets and critics. The subtext of *Finnegans Wake* contained a brief for the New Critical aesthetic: "[Joyce's] procedure . . . indicate[s] that the intention of art is in reaction against the processes of science, and that it wants to set up an object which is different in metaphysical kind from the objects scrutinized by science" (428).

Ransom excused the illogic and incoherence of *Finnegans Wake* as evidence of a higher artistic purpose. Ransom noted quite correctly that the operative principle in *Finnegans Wake* "punctually alters the terms of discourse as soon as discourse has started, and brings its effectiveness to an end" ("Aesthetic" 425). This he construed as a reaction to the progressive values of a science-oriented society. Joyce was not a nihilist or a Dadaist, for there was design, intention, and meaning in his experimentation; nor was he a primitivist, seeking some "return" to a purer, more primitive art. His book resembled a surreal or abstract painting, which "seems to intend to render genuine fragments of finished objects, but assembles them in confusion as if to say that these pieces of life will never add up into a whole" (427). The "disorderly energies" of the sections of the book moved it centrifugally, toward greater dissociation; the language, highly allusive, strained for "maximum connotation."

Out of the disorder of the *Wake*, Ransom could identify several elements that were coherent and conspicuous. He noted Joyce's use of verse jingles, his "ubiquitous sexual interest," and "the large solid blocks of Irish talk and Irish life, the biggest creative achievement in a work that is largely satirical, nonsensical, and negative" (427). These were some of the discernible parts of the abstract

composition entitled *Finnegans Wake*. They led Ransom
to praise Joyce's ear for language: "Doubtless no other
man lived with Joyce's sensibility for the poetic values or
the joke-values that depend on pure phonetic associations
of a given word" (426).

Ransom valued *Finnegans Wake* as a prose form that
approximated verse, one that could instruct poets "how
to escape from conceptual prose . . . into the contingent
world" (428). One of the objects of poetry was to create
logical discontinuities in order to establish a method of
perception that differed from scientific models. Nondis-
cursive art might violate rules of just proportion and
reverse the order of cause and effect. Ransom—and,
according to Ransom, Joyce—raised "irresponsibility"
and "irrelevance" into an art form. "[*Finnegans Wake*] is a
lesson book for aestheticians. If Joyce's art is almost completely irresponsible, any poem is, and by definition
should be, bent on introducing into discourse something
of what prose defines as irrelevance" (428). How different
a meaning the term "irresponsible" assumed for Archibald MacLeish one year later, when he used it to attack
the preciousness and self-indulgence of modernist art.

Ransom's qualified praise of *Finnegans Wake* in 1939
was an indication that his valuation of modernism was
changing. Indeed, in the 1940s, he joined Tate and
Brooks in their new enthusiasm for modernist art. While
he retained vestiges of his reactionary social and political
views, he embraced an art that, he argued, corroborated
his own political and social prejudices. The artist's quarrel
with society was an ancient and ongoing one, Ransom
implied, apparent in a classical poem as well as in the
most experimental of modernist works.

The views of R. P. Blackmur were influenced by the work of the New Critics, but his inclusion in this chapter is not meant to suggest that he belonged to the same family. His critical methods were similar to those of Tate and Ransom. He paid excruciatingly close attention to technical matters in his criticism, which, like Tate's and Ransom's, more often dealt with poetry than fiction. Paraphrasing Blackmur himself, Charles Glicksberg described Blackmur's criticism as "proceed[ing] on a rational plane, the plane, as he puts it, of competent technical analysis and appreciation, testing every judgment by the examination of minute particulars" (379). Blackmur was a conscientious student of literary form, and he faulted literature—D. H. Lawrence's poetry, for example—that placed a higher value on self-expression than on disciplined structure. He enthroned the rational intellect as the master of poetic and critical discourse.

Blackmur differed considerably from the New Critics in his political views. During the 1930s, he expressed general sympathy for Malcolm Cowley's fellow-traveling political opinions, though he rejected the use of Marxism as a critical method. As a critic, aesthetic questions occupied his full attention. He objected to the encroachment of ethical and political concerns into artistic judgments and criticized both Babbitt's Humanists and Hicks's Marxists for creating in the thirties an "air of witch-hunting and exorcism" (*Anni Mirabiles* 49). His commentaries on *Ulysses*, published in 1943 and 1956, were dense, difficult exegeses of the novel's themes and structure. Blackmur's convoluted style, which Kazin called "an unconscious travesty of [Henry] James's density and circumlocutionary wisdom" (*Native Grounds* 439), did not entirely obscure his admiration for *Ulysses*.

Blackmur's most extensive comments on *Ulysses* appeared in his 1943 essay, "The Jew in Search of a Son: Joyce's *Ulysses*," and in a lecture entitled "Reason in the Madness of Letters," delivered in 1956 at the Library of Congress. Though the lecture excerpt was for the most part a brief reiteration of the earlier essay, it also presented a clearer and more coherent defense of Joyce's work. Rejecting the notion that modernism was an "aberration" that would not sustain popular attention, Blackmur asserted that *Ulysses* was not "pure expressionism" but "a rational and traditional art" (*Anni Mirabiles* 42). It was a difficult and demanding work, but not indecipherable or chaotic. To examine the novel closely was to see that it "is the most structured book in English since at least Milton and it does as much to maintain and develop the full language as anybody since Shakespeare." Blackmur elaborated the "triple means" that made the novel work:

[Joyce's] basic patterns are universal and are known without their names. His chief characters are interesting and alive and parallel and completing to each other. And he had a story that is gradually told in immense bursts of vivid detail good whether or not there was a story at all; the detail makes the sense of the story. What unified these means is his always availing power to raise the language to the condition of glory or beauty. (*Anni Mirabiles* 42)

Evident in Blackmur's enthusiasm was his characteristic attention to language and structure and his clear desire to portray the novel as a more or less traditional narrative, with lifelike characters and a detailed plot. His was fundamentally an effort to demystify the novel.

The title of his earlier essay, "The Jew in Search of a Son," suggests that here, too, he was engaged in such an effort. He addressed the primary dramatic action, the twin quests that were central to the novel: Bloom's search for a son, and Stephen's search for a father. Stephen remained an "impossible" person, blasphemous, unyielding, in great need of Bloom as a corrective; on the other hand, Bloom, "the everlasting hero of the quotidian," "has no need to become anybody" (*Anni Mirabiles* 43). Bloom was the creative force in the novel, enterprising, accepting, hopeful, "the man infatuated with life" (*Anni Mirabiles* 44). Although Blackmur's reading seems clichéd to contemporary readers, and although he showed an irritating penchant for abstraction and allegory in his essay, he presented an interpretation of *Ulysses* that humanized and normalized a challenging and unusual book. His intention was to bridge what he referred to as the "gap" between the novel and the common reader.

Unlike Ransom in his reading of *Finnegans Wake*, Blackmur viewed *Ulysses* as a reflection of rather than a reaction to a disordered modern world. Joyce had rejected the rituals and hierarchy of the Catholic church, had spurned the dogma of political rhetoric, and had exploded literary conventions. What he presented in *Ulysses* was an arbitrary aesthetic order, replete with parody and heaps of naturalistic detail, that only underscored the chaotic nature of the world he portrayed. "No more orderly book of fiction was ever written, and no book in which the principles of order, unless taken aesthetically, seemed so frivolous or impotent. . . . Joyce. . . presented a kind of nihilism of unreasonable order" (*Eleven Essays* 32). The arbitrary and excessive aesthetic ordering of the universe of *Ulysses* confirmed, paradoxically, the absence of any true or abiding order in the world the novel depicted.

Blackmur's reading of Joyce differed in important ways from those of Tate, Ransom, and Brooks. In his desire to render *Ulysses* comprehensible to the general reader, Blackmur revealed a social conscience that was virtually absent in the commentaries of the others. Likewise, his affection for Bloom and his disdain for Stephen were a reversal of Brooks's sympathies and pointed again to a different political consciousness. He was as concerned with and as awed by the language of *Ulysses* as Brooks, but Blackmur, more than Brooks, discussed the novel in a social and historical context. Blackmur's critical method may indeed have owed a great deal to the New Critics, prompting Alfred Kazin to accuse him and them of a "violent narrowness of spirit" that created a "monstrous . . . criticism" (*Native Grounds* 439–40), but the affinities and the excesses to which Kazin alluded are not what are most apparent in Blackmur's comments on Joyce.

This survey of the responses to Joyce by the New Critics suggests that, unlike their intellectual adversaries in the 1930s from the left and the right, they evaluated Joyce's work according to aesthetic rather than political or ethical criteria. They admired Joyce primarily for his craftsmanship and his technical sophistication; they applauded the difficulty and equivocation of his work and the absence in it of cant. In most respects, he exemplified for them the artist dedicated to the same aesthetic ideals as they. They regarded Joyce's art as decidedly highbrow, a suitable challenge to the exegetical skills of formalist critics. Still, as Ransom demonstrated in his critique of *Finnegans Wake*, they read a political import in the Joycean aesthetic. Ransom in particular saw in *Finnegans Wake* a repudiation of the values and assumptions of Western liberalism and positivism. He admired not only the craft of the *Wake* but its implicit themes as well.

In many respects, the New Critics were the ideal readers of Joyce. In technical matters they were equal to the challenge presented by his work. They scrutinized the Joyce text with deliberateness and detachment, acutely, painstakingly aware of the nuances of language and the intricacies of form. They were the dedicated readers that Joyce, the maker of labyrinths, demanded. Perhaps too, they were the kind of readers that he most loved to tease, beguile, and even ridicule. For if the New Critics listened intently to the voice of the Joyce text, they invariably heard the one that sounded most like their own. They heard the voice of the shrewd and ironic artificer rather than the commonsensical, slightly sentimental citizen; the voice of self-righteousness and contempt rather than the voice of humility and compassion; the voice of self-imposed exile rather than the voice of reconciliation; the voice of Joyce/Stephen rather than the voice of Joyce/Bloom. In their obsessive research into the letter of Joyce, they missed something of his spirit, his humor, and his humanity; they failed to account adequately for those tentative and oblique affirmations that he offers in the pages of *Ulysses*. Richard Poirier notes that these omissions were evident in the New Critics' treatment of writers besides Joyce:

A lot of the joy of *Ulysses* and Faulkner, a lot of the hilarious revelation in Beckett of how conversation spins out of mere lassitude and inattention, not out of a questing for God—most of this was lost to students educated in the belief that if they worked grimly enough on modernist "difficulty," they could come back with Big Meanings, having touched the nerve centers of modern devaluation and cultural despair. (24)

A balanced evaluation of the New Critics' contribution to Joyce criticism must acknowledge not only the subtlety and ingenuity of their insights but the limited range of their vision as well.

The effect of their efforts is, however, less disputable. Although they did not give Joyce the attention they might have, they fostered a criticism that set the substance and tone for much of the Joyce criticism that followed. What today has become a Joyce industry consists almost entirely of exegetical analyses of the sort pioneered by the New Critics. Hugh Kenner, the most eminent Joyce critic writing today, acknowledged the debt owed by contemporary critics to the New Critics: "What the New Criticism did was return the study of literature—of poetry, primarily—to the central American intellectual concern, which is Language" ("Pedagogue as Critic" 41). In so doing, the New Critics wrested power away from the leftist ideologues of the thirties, whose efforts to distill the ideological content of literature were made to appear crude and misguided. The New Critics began the process of extricating Joyce's work from the crossfire of cultural politics in order to place it instead within the confines of the academy. The focus of critical debate over the Joyce text shifted from its social and political effects to its complex structure and style. Joyce became less of a cultural threat and more of a technical problem. And the attention he has received from the academy represents something of a fulfilled wish for the author himself, who, after the completion of *Ulysses*, predicted that his seven years of labor would keep the scholars busy for hundreds more. Today, Joyce's words from 1923 sound more prophetic than facetious: "I've put in so many enigmas and puzzles that it will keep the professors busy for centuries arguing over what I meant, and that's the only way of insuring one's immortality."[3]

5

The High Priest of Their Imagination: Joyce and His Catholic Critics

Actually, I have never known anyone with a mind so fundamentally Catholic in structure as Joyce's own, or one on whom the Church, its ceremonies, symbols, and theological declarations had made such an impress. . . . The Scholastic was the only philosophy he had ever considered seriously.   MARY COLUM, 1947

Even in his "overturning". . . Joyce has remained a pious Catholic. His "counter-world" has the medieval, quite provincial, and quintessentially Catholic atmosphere of an Erin that tries desperately to enjoy its political independence. The author worked at *Ulysses* in many foreign lands and from all of them he looked back in faith and kinship upon Mother Church and Ireland.   CARL JUNG, 1949

There can be no doubt that in *Finnegans Wake* Joyce is on the side of the devils. His use of the materials of orthodoxy should not be misconstrued. He uses them in the same way that Marx uses Hegel and the devil quotes Scripture.   J. MITCHELL MORSE, 1959

I confess I have no better explanation to offer of his triumphant struggle to preserve his rectitude as an artist in the midst of illness and disappointment, in abject poverty and disillusionment, than this, that he who has loved God intensely in his youth will never love anything less. The definition may change, the service abides.

STANISLAUS JOYCE, 1958

Joyce's attitude toward the Christian religion was twofold: when he remembered his own youthful conflict with it in its Irish-Roman form he could be bitterly hostile, but in general, viewing it as a whole as an objective reality and as epitomized human experience, and from a position well out of reach of any church's authority and sanctions it was for him a rich mine of material for the construction of his own myth.   FRANK BUDGEN, 1956

For Catholic readers in particular, and for many devout Christians as well, Joyce's work has posed a host of obvious problems. Joyce's portrayal of the Church and the priesthood was often sardonic, especially in his early work, *Dubliners* and *A Portrait of the Artist as a Young Man*. While Joyce demonstrated a fascination for the power and the mystery of Church ritual and doctrine, Catholicism was represented in his early books largely as a corrupt and oppressive force in Irish life, as the center of the center of paralysis. Joyce's rebellion against the Church was epitomized in the struggles of Stephen Dedalus, who rejected the priesthood and dedicated himself high-mindedly to an artistic career, to a "mode of life or of art whereby [my] spirit could express itself in unfettered freedom" (*Portrait* 246). His blasphemies against the Church in *Portrait* and in *Ulysses* were provocation enough for some Catholics, who considered Stephen to be a spokesman for Joyce and dismissed *Portrait* as an anti-Catholic tract.

There were other elements in Joyce's work that deeply troubled Catholic literary critics. Joyce's absorption in the quotidian details of Dublin life created a fictional world in which God seemed to be an irrelevance. Joyce's Dublin was a mass of detail, event, and characters in motion, a frenzied atmosphere unregulated by any higher spiritual authority and seemingly unjudged by any literary one. Joyce was regarded as a materialist and a sensualist, even a pornographer, a chronicler as well as a victim of the decay of modern life. Aside from Stephen's outright challenges to religious authority, perhaps what was most distressing to earnest believers was Joyce's comic sensibility. As Edwin Muir explained in 1926, it may have been Joyce's comic disposition that provoked not only religious readers but political ideologues as well.

Mr. Joyce tries to set in the plane of low comedy . . . professional seriousness of all kinds, and secondly the objects about which people are serious in this way: religion, to which the comic reaction is blasphemy; patriotism, to which it is little less; literature, to which it is parody; the claims of science, to which it is an application of anti-climax; sex, to which it is obscenity. . . . To see religion with the eyes of comedy is not, of course, to laugh it out of existence, any more than to see sex comically is to destroy it. All that comedy can destroy is strictly the second-rate. (30–31)

Muir does not suggest, as more superficial readers of Joyce have, that a comic treatment of religious issues destroys religious values or makes Joyce antireligious. A comic spirit may actually disguise serious religious belief and may in fact be the basis for a profound religious sensibility. Some Catholic readers have argued that Joyce's manifest protests against the Church obscured latent affinities with Catholic values and beliefs. Such, at least, is the claim made of the mature Joyce by L. A. G. Strong, Kristian Smidt, Robert Boyle, and others examined in this chapter.

Gauging the religious import of Joyce's work is as difficult as assessing Joyce's politics. The ambivalence, the contradiction, and the ambiguity that characterize so much of Joyce's thought make it impossible to reduce to easy theory or formula. Superficial, sentimental, or polemical analyses do little to elucidate the complexity of his attitudes. Although there is ostensible evidence to support a condemnatory reading such as Paul Elmer More's, Catholic readers of Joyce have labored mightily to establish the view that he was not a blasphemer or an atheist or a pornographer. In fact, Catholic readers of Joyce have endeavored to prove that Joyce never eluded the grasp of the Church, that he incorporated into his work Church ritual and dogma, and that he evolved a vision of the means and ends of human life that was profoundly affected by his religious training and vestigial religious values. During the last thirty years, Catholic critics have amplified T. S. Eliot's claim that Joyce's work was "penetrated with Christian feeling" (*Strange Gods* 48). L. A. G. Strong, Fr. William T. Noon, Fr. Robert Boyle and others have argued that Joyce, in his later years, returned to the faith he had tried to abandon, that his well-documented sundering was followed by a less apparent reconciliation, and that we ought to read *Ulysses* and *Finnegans Wake* as the expressions of a preeminently Catholic mind and sensibility.

Underlying much of the commentary on Joyce by Catholic critics was a veiled, and sometimes not so veiled, polemic. In the shadow of many of their textual explications were appropriative designs: they were eager to read in Joyce some confirmation or repudiation of their own religious views. The question was not whether Joyce's fiction could be admitted into the canon of great literature, but whether his work proved that he was among the saved or the damned. The portraits of the artist that emerge from such inquiries are as illuminating for what they reveal of the aims of some of his critics as for what they tell us of the range and complexity of the artist.

But the influence on Joyce criticism consists of more than a mission of Catholic scholars uncovering the latent Catholicism in Joyce's work. The conjoining of a religious orthodoxy to reactionary political views has had an even greater impact on the portraits of Joyce drawn by two of his most important readers, T. S. Eliot and Hugh Kenner. Like Tate, Ransom, and Brooks, who were Eliot's literary comrades-in-arms and Kenner's teachers, Eliot and Kenner embraced modernist aesthetics without sacrificing their deeply held religious beliefs or their political conservatism.[1] What allied Eliot and the New Critics was an aversion to the industrialization and democratization of modern life. Their religious convictions formed the basis for a social critique: they found modern American life to be crassly materialistic, dehumanizing, spiritually arid, and culturally stultifying. Religion was a necessary link to the past in a rapidly changing world as well as a necessary "check" on the pretentiousness and moral levity of a liberal capitalist society. Moreover, wrote Eliot, religion was an essential condition for the development of culture: "The only hopeful course for a society which would thrive and continue its creative activity in the arts of civilization, is to become Christian. That project involves, at least, discipline, inconvenience, and discomfort: but here as hereafter the alternative to hell is purgatory" (*Christian Society* 19).

For Eliot and the New Critics, and later for Kenner, religious convictions were indispensable in shaping a reactionary social perspective, from which the spectacle of modern civilization appeared as a living hell. Such a weltanschauung drove Eliot and the New Critics toward the safe confines of aesthetic form and colored their critical judgments as well. In the case of New Critical commentary on Joyce, we remarked how Ransom, most notably, sought corroboration of his own social biases in his reading of *Finnegans Wake*. Eliot and Kenner discovered between the lines of Joyce's work the disposition of a moralizing Christian. Kenner in particular saw in Joyce the calculating eye of a vigilant and severe judge of his fellowman. Both implied that beneath the manifest anti-Catholicism in Joyce's fiction lay a residue of Catholic belief and sensibility; both saw in Joyce a figure bearing a marked resemblance to themselves.

In his widely read tribute to *Ulysses*, "*Ulysses*, Order, and Myth," Eliot praised Joyce's use of the "mythical method" as a means of representing contemporary life. "I hold this book to be the most important expression which the present age has found," Eliot declared; "it is a book to which we are all indebted, and from which none of us can escape" (198). Joyce's incorporation of the Homeric epic allowed him to bridge the gap between the classical and the modern worlds and to give an ordered frame to the chaotic experience of modern life. Eliot disputed the notion that *Ulysses* presented a distorted picture of everyday life or that the novel was libelous to humanity. Joyce's stroke of genius had the significance of a scientific breakthrough. *Ulysses*, quite simply, "[made] the modern world possible for art."

In using the myth, in manipulating a continuous parallel between contemporaneity and antiquity, Mr. Joyce is pursuing a
method which others must pursue after him. . . . It is simply a
way of controlling, of ordering, of giving a shape and a significance to the immense panorama of futility and anarchy which
is contemporary history. . . . Instead of the narrative method,
we may now use the mythical method. It is, I seriously believe,
a step toward making the modern world possible for art, toward that order and form which Mr. Aldington so earnestly
desires. (201–2)

Eliot's enthusiasm for Joyce's "mythical method" was
founded on Eliot's fear of and thorough contempt for the
conditions of modern life. It was a contempt which he
too readily assumed Joyce shared. Eliot argued that the
Homeric parallels in *Ulysses* gave a shape and structure to
the disorder of contemporary life. Other readers, including Ezra Pound, argued that the Odyssean correspon-
dences played a less important role in the novel. Pound
maintained that they provided Joyce with a necessary
scaffolding to construct the edifice of the novel but they
were clearly subordinate to the novel's action.[2] In fact, references to the *Odyssey* are more muted and less frequent
in the later episodes of *Ulysses*, in "Circe," "Ithaca," and
"Penelope." Edmund Wilson believed that the mythic
parallels, along with other allusions and interpolations,
were flaws in the novel that slowed the narrative movement and were symptomatic of the author's obsessive,
"supernormally energetic" mind (*Axel's Castle* 215). The
Italian Marxist Franco Moretti maintains that Eliot's enthusiasm for Joyce's "mythical method" explains much
more about Eliot than it does about Joyce. Eliot, Moretti
argues, valued myth as a way to mold history, to create

an ordered and predictable future. Joyce, on the other
hand, did not privilege myth as Eliot did. "Joyce uses
myth only to desecrate it, and through it, to desecrate
contemporary history: to parody Bloom with Ulysses,
and Ulysses with Bloom; to create an order which gives
greater relief to the absence of order, a nucleus gone hay-
wire with irony and distortions" (192). For Moretti's
Joyce, myth could not be equated with aesthetic form, as
it could for Eliot; it "therefore cannot be the starting
point for a new cultural hegemony" (192).

Eliot's gaze held fixedly to the myth rather than to the
matter of *Ulysses*; it was by reference to the myth that the
matter was to be judged. But Eliot's novel was not
Joyce's. Modern life and the consciousness of modern
man were not mercilessly satirized in *Ulysses*, or not satirized only. Both were explored and celebrated with pains-
taking care and detail. Moreover, Joyce's major achievement in the novel, one unremarked by Eliot, was the
largely sympathetic treatment given to its protagonist, a
middle-class Jew named Bloom. Bloom is the object of
our affection and laughter, our pity and respect. He does
not simply suffer from comparisons with his mythological counterpart but emerges as something of a hero himself. He is the epitome of modern man and the product of
the modern age. Eliot might have agreed with Ezra
Pound's description: "Bloom very much *is* the mess"
(Deming 2:215).

Eliot could only accept the social world of *Ulysses* by
assuming that Joyce was making a judgment against it;
his own social vision differed so fundamentally from
Joyce's egalitarian sentiments or from Bloom's schemes
for social reform. Eliot's politics were unabashedly elitist:
"The governing elite. . . would consist of those whose

responsibility was inherited with their affluence and position, and whose forces were constantly increased, and often led, by rising individuals of exceptional talents" (*Notes* 159). Privilege, stability, discipline, reverence for God and tradition, homogeneity of race and religion were the hallmarks of Eliot's social vision. A "spirit of excessive tolerance is to be deprecated," he warned in *After Strange Gods* (1933); "and reasons of race and religion combine to make any large number of free-thinking Jews undesirable" (20). In *The Idea of a Christian Society* (1939), Eliot inveighed against the evils of democratic liberalism and warned of its consequences:

By destroying traditional social habits of the people, by dissolving their natural collective consciousness into individual constituents, by licensing the opinions of the most foolish, by substituting instruction for education, by encouraging cleverness rather than wisdom, the upstart rather than the qualified, by fostering a notion of *getting on* to which the alternative is a hopeless apathy, Liberalism can prepare the way for that which is its own negation: the artificial, mechanised or brutalised control which is a desperate remedy for its chaos. (12)

It is indeed a remarkable feat that one with so thoroughly reactionary a perspective as Eliot could find anything praiseworthy in *Ulysses*.

Ulysses was not the only work of Joyce's that Eliot held in high regard. In "A Message to the Fish" (1941) he referred to "The Dead" as "one of the finest short stories in the language" (468), citing it to rebut claims that Joyce devalued nature and the human spirit. In *After Strange Gods* (1933) he showed himself so moved by the story that he declared Joyce to be "the most ethically orthodox

of the more eminent writers of my time" (38). Eliot's
assessment was based not on the author's professed beliefs but on his "orthodoxy of sensibility" and his "sense
of tradition." Although Eliot admired the elaborate and
allusive structure of "The Dead," he was most absorbed
with Gabriel Conroy's struggle with his own conscience.
Gabriel is humbled following his wife's admission of
passion for young Michael Furey. Gabriel's pretentiousness, his self-centeredness, and his superficiality are exposed, and he becomes a penitent sinner at the story's
close. Undoubtedly, it was Gabriel's epiphanic moment of
self-revelation and repentance and his subsequent unifica-
tion with "all the living and the dead" that moved Eliot
to declare at the end of his essay: "I consider Mr. Joyce's
work to be penetrated with Christian feeling" (48). Modern man, Eliot insisted, needs to "restore the sense of
Original Sin" (42) and reengage himself, as Gabriel Conroy had, with the struggle for his own soul. He must
divest himself of romantic, post-Enlightenment illusions
and cast a cold eye on the godless idealism of a liberal and
progressive age.

   Eliot's admiration for Joyce was based on what Eliot
regarded as Joyce's deep-seated religious sensibility and
Joyce's use of classical literature in his depiction of contemporary life. Eliot's Joyce possessed the "historical
sense," which, he explained in "Tradition and the Individual Talent" (1919), "compels a man to write not merely
with his own generation in his bones, but with a feeling that the whole of literature of Europe from Homer
and within it the whole of the literature of his own country has a simultaneous existence and composes a simultaneous order" (*Essays* 4). Moreover, Joyce appeared to
embody the ideal of the impersonal artist so central to

Eliot's aesthetic theory. Eliot inveighed against the cult of individualism and personality in art, a condition he regarded as symptomatic of a culture bereft of a religious and literary tradition. "The poet has, not a 'personality' to express, but a particular medium, which is only a medium and not a personality, in which impressions and experiences combine in peculiar and unexpected ways" (*Essays* 9). Eliot's Joyce was this perfect medium, seemingly detached, antididactic, blending past and present. The meaning of *Ulysses* was not in any transparent authorial message but in the juxtaposition of myth and modernity, the order of the past a counterpoint to the chaos of the present. Eliot fashioned a Joyce in conformity with his own standards and sensibility. In the process, he deftly executed his critical mission, which on one occasion he defined in this way: "There are standards of criticism, not ordinarily in use, which we may apply to whatever is offered to us as works of philosophy or of art, which might help to render them safer and more profitable for us" (*Strange Gods* 63).

Eliot's reading of Joyce resonates in Hugh Kenner's first major contribution to Joyce scholarship, *Dublin's Joyce* (1956), though of course Kenner's book offers a much more extensive treatment of Joyce's fiction than Eliot's essays. Kenner assiduously traces the sourcebooks of Joyce's works, painstakingly examines the language of *Ulysses*, and attempts to locate Joyce's oeuvre within a modern context of moral, philosophical, and political change. Like Eliot, Kenner reads Joyce's work as an indictment of the various "isms" that constitute contemporary culture: liberalism, individualism, materialism, and aestheticism. Also, as in the case of Eliot, Kenner's early remarks on Joyce reveal a great deal about Kenner's own temperament, religious beliefs, and social prejudices. Whereas Eliot saw Joyce as both a classicist and an aesthetic innovator, with kindred fascist sympathies, Kenner's Joyce emerges as a thoroughgoing ironist and irrepressible moralist. Saturating the pages of *Dublin's Joyce* is a tone of persistent scolding, Kenner reminding us always of the stasis and awful corruption that reigns over Joyce's Irish wasteland. Kenner implies, and occasionally states outright, that Joyce, too, sits in judgment over his city of dead souls. Brilliant as Kenner's insights are, influential as they have been, his signature is indelibly etched in his skewed portrait of Joyce in *Dublin's Joyce*.

Despite the persistent moralism in *Dublin's Joyce*, Kenner demonstrates an acute sensitivity to Joyce's use of language, though this is even more in evidence in *Joyce's Voices* (1978), a deft analysis of Joyce's stylistic techniques in *Ulysses*. In *Dublin's Joyce*, Kenner argues that Joyce's true subject in *Ulysses* is Dublin's language, in which is preserved the only vitality of a dead city and its dead citizenry.[3] Cued by Joyce's portrait of Dublin, Kenner sees a vista of sordidness and corruption, which he evokes in images of death, catatonia, and inebriation:

[In *Ulysses*] Joyce embalms in cadences what Dublin embalms in music, and entraps in the amber of learned multiple puns the futile vigour which the Dubliner, gazing into his peat-colored Guinness, must generate in language because its counterpart has slipped out of life. (12)

[In *Finnegans Wake*] Joyce projects in language the generic Dubliner's image: a cataleptic dreaming of the waking world, all his reality a dream and a dream made out of words, the stones of Dublin, its smells, its sunlight, everything but its language taken away. (18)

This is the world of Eliot's Hollow Men, a somnambulatory universe in which nothing changes, in which man is stripped of dignity and potency, in which life lacks meaning or value. "Everything has become all that it can ever be, the past is exhausted. . . nothing can be willed away, nothing can change, nothing is of the slightest intrinsic interest, and that is hell" (238). *Finnegans Wake* only appears to offer a reprieve from the catalogues of dead objects and deadened spirits heaped in *Ulysses*; but, claims Kenner, "the relation between Bloom's day and Earwicker's night is analogous with the relation between infernal and purgatorial states" (239).

Kenner's perspective on Joyce does in some dimensions dovetail with Eliot's, but it may owe even more to the views of Wyndham Lewis, whose essay on Joyce Kenner admired, with some qualifications.[4] Although his response to *Ulysses* was more sympathetic than Lewis's, Kenner shared Lewis's revulsion for modern life. Both abhorred the Philistinism, the vulgarity, and the amorality chronicled in the pages of *Ulysses*. In Kenner's mind, the path toward progressivism and materialism was, again, the route to hell:

To cast the doctor as priest is to strike at the outset the note of materialistic transposition that runs throughout the book. The body usurps the room of the soul, theology gives way to associationist psychology, visions become hallucinations, the metaphors of Scripture receive bitterly literal realization in matter, in an inferno whose apotheosis is the debris-crammed brain of hapless Leopold Bloom. (*Dublin's Joyce* 230)

ysses (107), but Kenner, like Eliot,
found a way to hold his nose and smile knowingly,
approvingly. Lewis, Kenner argued, was too engaged in
a polemical tug-of-war to notice that Joyce, the chap at
the end of the line who appeared to be paring his fingernails, was actually tugging gently and discreetly on
Lewis's side of the knot.

Kenner congratulates Lewis for three essential insights
into *Ulysses* that potentially could have served as "master
keys" for a "definitive exegesis" of the novel: (1) the
novel's characters are clichés; (2) Stephen is a "hopeless
farce" (364); and (3) the book shows an unprecedented
concern with the "flux of matter" (363), or, in Lewis's
veiled excremental metaphor, a "physical enthusiasm that
expresses itself in [a] tremendous outpouring of matter,
or stuff" (Lewis 109). The latter, according to both Kenner and Lewis, results in a plodding and mechanical
movement in the novel that mirrors the mechanization
and spiritual deadness of modern Dublin. The authorial
intelligence behind the "huge and intricate machine" of
Ulysses is itself mechanical: "craftsmanlike and unreflec-
tive, gifted at transcription, with minimal distortion . . . a
thinking machine, in short, the incarnation of quasi-
industrial 'know-how,'" according to Kenner (*Dublin's
Joyce* 167), "not so much an inventive intelligence as an
executant," according to Lewis (quoted in *Dublin's Joyce*
167). But Lewis errs, says Kenner, in identifying this per-
sona with Joyce. This is the author's fabrication, behind
which Joyce stands, indifferently paring his fingernails.

It is essential to the total effect of *Ulysses* that it should seem to
be the artifact of a mind essentially like Bloom's, only less
easily deflected; a mind that loses nothing, penetrates nothing,

and has a category for everything; the mind that at length epiphanizes itself in the catechism of "Ithaca.". . . It is by the insane mechanical meticulousness of that mode of consciousness, the mode of consciousness proper to industrial man, that in *Ulysses* industrial man is judged. *That* is, in a way, the "meaning" of the book, the form in which it remains as a whole in the memory. One of Joyce's greatest creations is the character of this sardonic impersonal recorder, that constantly glints its photoelectric eyes from behind the chronicle of Bloomsday. (*Dublin's Joyce* 168)

For Kenner, this "sardonic impersonal recorder" is the embodiment of industrial man and becomes the means by which we judge that man and his era. It is also, according to Kenner, the source of laughter in the novel. We laugh *at* it, as a "monstrous parody" of the workings of the "super-brain" (168); and we also laugh, if occasionally through our tears, *with* it, at the desiccated landscape it surveys. This is another manifestation of "double-writing," or the multiple layering of meaning and perspective that Kenner is ceaselessly explicating in Joyce's writing.

Kenner insists, more emphatically than Lewis, that the Stephen Dedalus of *Portrait* and *Ulysses* not be confused with his creator, James Joyce. Stephen is culpable of a host of sins and, even more than Bloom, is subject to severe moral scrutiny from Joyce. Joyce's ironic distance saves him from Kenner's censure: it is Stephen, not Joyce, who is a blasphemer and a deluded romantic. "Joyce was never the Stephen Dedalus of his 1914 *Portrait*, mirror of nineteenth-century romantic idealism" (*Dublin's Joyce* 114). The romantic tradition, of which Stephen is the culmination, creates isolates, exiles, and megalomaniacs. It does not lead toward either personal or artistic fulfillment. Stephen, like his mythological namesake, is bound to fall, precisely because he repudiates his "fallen" condition. "Stephen does not, as the careless reader may suppose, become an artist by rejecting church and country. Stephen does not become an artist at all. Country, church, and mission are an inextricable unity, and in rejecting the two that seem to hamper him, he rejects also the one on which he has set his heart" (*Dublin's Joyce* 160). Kenner argues that it is pure romantic foolishness to assume one can mature personally and artistically outside an institutional framework, free of bonds to nation or religion. As he does throughout *Dublin's Joyce*, Kenner reminds us that social and familial institutions— the city, the Church, the family—are not obstacles to meaning and fulfillment but the very means to achieve them.

Stephen is an ironic representation of the Ibsen hero, the social outcast who prides himself on his practice of "high unconsortability" as a mode of living (*Dublin's Joyce* 160). Kenner argues that Joyce exorcised the demon of Ibsen by exposing the unfeasibility, the sheer ridiculousness of such a posture in the stories of Stephen Dedalus, Gabriel Conroy, and Richard Rowan.[5] Each of these characters wears the cloak of "ethical absolutism." They are brittle, humorless souls, ponderous social outcasts whom we would laugh at if, as Kenner says about Stephen, we didn't have the intuition that he was "a victim being prepared for a sacrifice" (132). Indeed, these eccentrics *are* sacrificed, by the sword of Joyce's irony, for the entrance of their worthier successor: communal man, first in the form of Bloom, then Earwicker and Anna Livia. "In *Finnegans Wake*," writes Kenner, "Joyce reversed for the western world that current that has flowed from Milton's exile myth into the romantic nightworld" (90). Joyce had served his apprenticeship to Ibsen, had "pierced the purple fog of Yeatsian aestheticism" (160) and was now under the tutelage of other masters: Homer, Vico, Lewis Carroll, and Sophocles.

[Ibsen] had never known, and could not know amid the frontier vacuum of the fiords, the traditions of the European community of richly-nourished life; and the lonely starvation of his ideal of free personal affinity in no context save that of intermingling wills inspired Joyce with a fascination that generated *Exiles* and a repulsion that found its objective correlative when Leopold Bloom, reversing Gabriel Conroy's lust for snow, shuddered beneath "the apathy of the stars." (94)

Bloom is the antipode to Stephen, and his virtue lies in his acceptance of the obligations imposed by a fractured family and community. He is Dr. Watson to Stephen's Sherlock Holmes, the social man to Stephen's outlaw, the man of compassion to the disembodied intellect. But Bloom, the "timid cuckold" (356), is hardly heroic, in Kenner's estimation. He is the epitome of the deracinated, undereducated, soulless, and impotent modern man. He is mocked by the Odyssean parallel: "Dublin an immense graveyard of buried hopes, heroic promises dead, promised Homeric heroisms shrunken to the fulfillment of a Bloom" (210). At times, Kenner can hardly contain his disgust for Bloom. He warns us that we ought not to sentimentalize Bloom or regard him as anything more than another member of the living dead: "Bloom is not entitled to sentimental regard as the champion of the plain man. He is the most inadequate Messiah imaginable" (256).

Molly comes in for even harsher reprobation. Kenner had found nothing salutary in Stephen and Bloom's unconscious revelations in the "Circe" episode and saw no

affirmation—or at least none worth praising—emerging
from Molly's monologue which closes the novel. Kenner
objects to sentimental readings of either episode and em-
ploys the term "animality" frequently in his discussion of
the characters and events in both. "Circe" he regards as
"an apocalypse climaxing in the Black Mass and the burn-
ing of Dublin" (259). Stephen's attempt to smash the
chandelier is no apotheosis: "All he does is epiphanize
his own Luciferian sin against the light" (260). Molly's
"yesses" threaded through "Penelope" demonstrate her
lack of self-restraint and her moral turpitude; they are
her passwords to hell—the destination to which all
of these unfortunate souls in the novel seem bound.
"[Molly's] 'Yes' of consent. . . kills the soul [and] has
darkened the intellect and moral sense of all Dublin. . . .
Her 'Yes' is confident and exultant; it is the 'Yes' of
authority: authority over this animal kingdom of the
dead" (262).

Kenner takes special pride in distinguishing himself
from those he considers sentimental readers of Joyce. In
Dublin's Joyce he poses as a relentless moralist, a tough-
minded interpreter of a shrewd and elusive author. Kenner's Joyce is not Stephen/Joyce, not a blasphemer, not a
pornographer, not supremely indifferent to the decay of
Western civilization. Kenner objects to the cultic idoliza-
tion of Joyce for virtues he was never truly guilty of:
"[Joyce] was praised for being Stephen Dedalus, smasher
of chandeliers, disgusted with everyone and everything;
which disgust insured his having no particular axes to
grind, like a white-coated Frankenstein, above politics,
devoted to pure science, standing behind the wreckage of
Hiroshima, inscrutable, paring his fingernails" (359). This
is not the portrait of the artist Kenner celebrates. Kenner
is much more sympathetic to Wyndham Lewis's perspec-

tive, which, Kenner maintains, is closer to the truth, in spite of its polemical excesses.

In Kenner's compact 1978 study, *Joyce's Voices*, language is still the subject and hero of *Ulysses*, but here Kenner displays little of the moralism so pervasive in his earlier book. Still concerned primarily with Joyce's manipulation of style, syntax, and diction in *Ulysses*, Kenner further demonstrates how Joyce moves from a style of "Objectivity" to a purposeful distortion of language in the later episodes, blocking our vision and obscuring our understanding. In moving away from narrative toward a preoccupation with style, Joyce progressively frustrates our desire to interpret, to render meaning. Kenner, who in his eclectic reach has appropriated deconstructionist theory, concludes *Joyce's Voices* by exposing the epistemological uncertainties that abound in the text of *Ulysses* and by insisting on the arbitrariness of its interpretation. The language of *Ulysses* conceals rather than reveals; truths are multiple; "the whole truth about even a circumscribed situation is probably uncommunicable" (*Joyce's Voices* 89). What a different book, what a different writer Joyce has become in the two decades since *Dublin's Joyce*! Moral judgments have been replaced by moral quandries; the ironist has become the artful dodger; the teller of painful truths has become the jokester who mocks the very notion of "truth." Kenner has ceased his moralizing, preferring instead to explicate the quirks and subtleties of style in *Ulysses*. The Catholic and reactionary sensibility that gave shape to *Dublin's Joyce* has receded before the linguist and aesthetic philosopher for whom the ascription of meaning is a perilous enterprise.

What links Eliot's essays and Kenner's first book on Joyce to Catholic exegeses is the assumption that beneath the impressive technical apparatus of Joyce's fiction lies a deep-seated and profoundly religious sensibility. Moreover, in spite of the manifest anti-Catholicism in Joyce's work (usually issuing from the mouth or mind of Stephen Dedalus) Joyce remained emotionally and psychologically attached to the Church. Kevin Sullivan writes that "Joyce never completely succeeded, nor does it appear that he ever wished to succeed, in severing those emotional and imaginative ties that bound him to his spiritual mother, the Church invisible" (54). Joyce's religious sensibility expressed itself in a variety of ways in his work, some more apparent than others. Incorporation of Catholic liturgy and scripture presents obvious examples, but Joyce also drew on Church ritual and dogma in a broader sense, using as the thematic substructure of his work, for example, the confessional, the celebration of communion between man and man and man and God, and the quest for redemption and salvation. Most Catholic readers argue that Joyce moved away from the naturalism and persistent irony in the early works toward myth and mysticism and a greater sense of compassion in *Ulysses* and *Finnegans Wake*. They point particularly to *Finnegans Wake* as evidence that Joyce had recovered or finally expressed latent religious sentiments and beliefs.

One of the central issues for religious readers of Joyce is the relationship between the artist and his alter-ego, Stephen Dedalus. Most Catholic commentators on Joyce have agreed with Hugh Kenner that Stephen is *not* Joyce, though some contend that Kenner exaggerates the distance between the two.[6] However, J. Mitchell Morse and Kristian Smidt, both writing in the late 1950s, argue that Stephen's aesthetic and religious opinions were essentially

Joyce's own. Morse argues that throughout his life Joyce remained an ambivalent Catholic at best, and that his work is noteworthy not for its reconciliation with the faith but for its unremitting struggle with the authority of the Church. Stephen's presumptuousness is Joyce's own.

Joyce, having found himself unable to subordinate intellect to faith, as Eliot did, or to seek virtue in degradation, as Baudelaire did, could free himself of the sense of sin as society understood it only by denying the concept of sin as society understood it, and establishing for himself, as godlike artist, a completely different scale of values. All his work is the record of a struggle to do this, to overcome the persistent influences of his upbringing. (Morse 22)

Joyce flouted the Jesuitical practice of self-renunciation, instead raising the artist to the level of the divine, knowing in his own tormented soul that he was risking damnation for it: "[Joyce's] terrible indictment. . . amounts to a denial of God in the name of the human individual, who cannot live with Him; it is, in fact, the obverse of the Jesuit denial of the individual self in the name of God" (Morse 80).

But as much as he struggled to do so, Joyce could never free himself of the grip of the Church. Morse makes the familiar argument about Joyce, that his compulsive rebelliousness represented a form of continuing intellectual dependence on Catholicism. In any case, Joyce was too self-conscious an artist and possessed too complex a mind to be able to renounce categorically his Jesuit upbringing or to deny the power and profundity of the Jesuits' view of life. Joyce could neither fully embrace nor completely reject his religious background; he remained suspended between sympathy and alienation. "Joyce's conscience is neither that of a conformist nor altogether that of a rebel, but the permanent uneasy conscience of an artist" (Morse 88).

A very different view of Joyce is taken by Kristian Smidt. While agreeing with Morse that Joyce's opinions corresponded with Stephen's, Smidt goes on to argue not only that Joyce's temperament was a profoundly religious one, but that Joyce was performing priestlike functions through his art. Joyce, like Stephen, was drawn early and powerfully to the Church, chiefly to the aura of mystery that surrounded it. Smidt agrees with Kevin Sullivan that, had family circumstances been different, Joyce could very well have become a priest. Instead, Joyce broke his ties with Church, family, and state and declared his allegiance to art, but as an artist he was haunted by what he had abandoned. In his imagination, he returned to Dublin, reconstituted a family, and "turned his art into a cult to replace Christianity and himself into its deity, its priest and its devotees in one person" (Smidt 27).

Joyce's "cult of art" was an individual rather than a communal rite that affirmed a transcendent realm of existence. Joyce worshipped two gods: himself, and the goddess of Beauty, epitomized by Molly Bloom and Anna Livia Plurabelle. Joyce himself and his alter-ego Stephen resembled Christ in the self-sacrifice and search for redemption in their creative work. Here and elsewhere, Smidt overlooks evidence contrary to his thesis and strains to make Joyce's temperament appear as religious as he claims.

Smidt's Joyce is not Kenner's ironist but a Blakean visionary and mystic. Joyce wished to create a counter-religion in his work in which nothing would be too base or too sublime for godlike artistic apprehension. In *Finnegans Wake* ("Allspace in a Notshall") and in such episodes as "Circe" in *Ulysses*, Joyce attempted to free himself from the constraints of time and space. While Kenner mocked such artistic pretension, and while Wyndham Lewis disparaged Joyce's immersion in the "time-flux," Smidt announces that Joyce not only sought but gained transcendence from the mundane and quotidian. Words were indeed Joyce's weapon, but for the purpose of spiritual rather than political enlightenment. Smidt maintains that words assumed an almost sacred meaning to Joyce and in their obscurity resembled a form of "ecstatic babbling" tantamount to speaking in tongues. This was an expression of Joyce's "mystical groping towards the divine."

The liturgy of the Catholic Church is an international language, and Joyce's language is international, though in a different way. The sense of mystery is aroused by his polyglot style because one feels that the underlying idea is that of an indivisible *Logos*. . . . It has the power to unite humanity by means of communication and raise it to a superhuman status. (70)

Joyce's ambitions were grandiose: *Ulysses* and *Finnegans Wake* were written to redeem a cursed and paralyzed Irish race. However, stepping back from his own grandiose appraisal of Joyce's artistic project, Smidt concedes, "[Joyce's] success in bringing about a spiritual regeneration of his country is doubtful, I suppose" (103).

Smidt's analysis of Joyce's work suffers most from overstatement and religious sentimentalization, and the portrait of the artist that emerges is less funny, less obscene, and much more solemn than that to which we are accustomed. Inevitably, Smidt either ignores or gives scant attention to the evidence contrary to his hypotheses, and he chastises Joyce for his intrusive parodies and "tricks of style" (102). He regards Joyce's humor as a counterimpulse to his cultic ambitions and as a way of masking the seriousness of his religious longing. "Joyce to a certain extent protected his solemnity against ridicule in his own mind and at the hands of his readers by presenting it as grotesque" (102). Smidt, like a shrewd psychoanalytic critic, transforms what appears to be contradictory evidence into support for his own thesis.

Kevin Sullivan's *Joyce Among the Jesuits* (1958) is more a biographical than a critical study, in which Sullivan concludes, from extensive research, that the Jesuits who were Joyce's teachers left an indelible stamp on the mind of the artist. Sullivan, like Robert Boyle and William T. Noon, is a Catholic scholar engaged in a literary reclamation project. He argues that, despite much evidence to the contrary, Joyce never left the faith that so early nurtured him. Sullivan, Boyle, and Noon make it very clear that Joyce was decidedly *not* Stephen Dedalus. Joyce was neither the heretic that Stephen was, nor was he "the philosophic idealist or solipsistic aesthete that Stephen Dedalus became" (82). In a judgment that reveals the critic more than it does Joyce, Sullivan claims, even more emphatically than Smidt, that had Joyce's social and familial environment been less "corrosive and contemptible . . . there would have been no deterioration in his relations with the Jesuits, no rejection of Catholicism, no abandonment of home and country, and possibly no *Portrait*—or at least a very different kind of portrait" (11). Nor, we are tempted to add, would there have been a James Joyce.

Sullivan explains Joyce's actual break with the Church

as a symbolic reenactment of the artist's oedipal conflict. Joyce's quarrel was really not with Catholicism but with his parents. His rejection of Catholicism was a rejection of his authoritarian father who, like the clergy, mediated between the son and the sacred object: on the one hand, the mother, on the other, God.

This separation was an intellectual act . . . by which Joyce cut himself off from the visible Church as manifest in the words and works of the priest or spiritual father; but Joyce never completely succeeded, nor does it appear that he ever wished to succeed, in severing those emotional and imaginative ties that bound him to his spiritual mother, the Church invisible. To this extent, at least, the Jesuits never lost their hold on Joyce, paradoxical as their hold on him may now appear. (54)

We are reminded here of Kristian Smidt's solemn efforts to rationalize Joyce's humor. Both Smidt and Sullivan maneuver ingeniously to support the thesis that Joyce remained deeply religious, but their efforts underscore the fact that Joyce's religious attitudes remained ambiguous and contradictory and cannot be understood by resort to stereotypes.

Sullivan, like Smidt, maintains that Joyce the artist was haunted by Joyce the priest, but Sullivan's artist is less ecumenical, more particularly Catholic. Joyce's work resembles an aestheticized form of the confessional, his characters, unrepentant sinners. The rituals and beliefs of the Church are the foundation stones of his fictions:

Joyce may have begun to live for literature, but he continued to live in doubt. It was because of this habitual doubt, plus the intensity of his adolescent temptation to the priesthood, that the shadow of the priest falls constantly across the work of the artist. So it is that in *Ulysses*, and even in *Finnegans Wake*, the shadow-structure is the Catholic Mass in which the priest, performing the specific sacrifice for which he was ordained, celebrates the communion of God and man. But the artist secularizes this function of the priest, and his sacrament is a celebration of the communion of humanity. (146)

Sullivan's claim of the enduring influence of the Jesuits on Joyce echoes in two critical studies of Joyce's work by Catholic scholars, Fr. William T. Noon's *Joyce and Aquinas* (1957) and Fr. Robert Boyle's *James Joyce's Pauline Vision: A Catholic Exposition* (1978). Both studies have the effect of softening Joyce's attitude toward Catholicism by demonstrating how Joyce used elements of the Thomistic or Pauline vision in developing his art. Both argue—Boyle more emphatically than Noon—that Joyce's art became a secular means of religious expression, and that the influence of Aquinas and Paul was instrumental in modifying Joyce's aesthetic theories to allow a fuller expression of his religious sensibility in *Ulysses* and especially in *Finnegans Wake*.

Noon believes that Aquinas drew Joyce away from Stephen's preoccupation with aesthetics in *Portrait*. *Ulysses*, unlike *Portrait*, acknowledges the limitations of man and art and redirects the concern of the artist away from abstract theorizing and toward the "'supra-social general commitment' of literature to existence" (58). Joyce resembles Gabriel Conroy in this respect more than he does Stephen Dedalus, for Gabriel moves beyond aestheticism and toward communion with his fellowman. The orientation of *Ulysses* is primarily social; it affirms conservative and traditional values in regard to family, sex, and politics. Although it is undeniably a critique of modern life, one finds throughout a comic and conciliatory tone: "Joyce succeeds in presenting a searching and exhaustive critique of contemporary society. . . [but] the tone of the novel is nowhere near that of *saeva indignatio*. Religious mores are satirized. . . sentimental patriotism is parodied, modern science is mocked. . . but at the same time there is an absence of anger" (101). Noon presents a balanced view of *Ulysses*: its author is neither a nihilist, a moralist, nor a romantic sentimentalist.

Noon argues that Aquinas's influence was critical in the evolution of Joyce's theory of epiphany. As he matured, the source of the epiphany shifted from actual experience to language. Words assumed multifarious symbolic meanings, particularly in the "metaphorical, metaphysical experimentation with language" in the *Wake* (158). Words became a way of capturing and contemplating the deepest mysteries of life. *Finnegans Wake* is more than a linguistic riddle: it is an implicit "avowal of personal faith. . . [which] revolves around a core of theological acceptance" (143). Aquinas the philosopher-theologian taught Joyce the artist that the poetic construct resembled the work of the God of creation and that words were both mysterious and sacred.

Robert Boyle presents a portrait of the artist as a Catholic mystic, similar in many respects to Kristian Smidt's view of Joyce. Boyle argues that Joyce used literature as Scripture by presenting a timeless vision beyond the ken of rational explanation. Artistic and religious fulfillment were analogous: both revealed the universality of experience and the deepest potential of the human soul. Such revelations occur in the final episodes of *Ulysses* and throughout *Finnegans Wake*. Joyce came to understand that the appeal of Catholicism lay in its transcendental aspirations and in its respect for the longing of the human spirit. "[Joyce] did not see Catholicism as simply an evil force frustrating and repressing the self. He did, of course, see that aspect, but he saw it against the background of Catholic aspiration to fulfill and complete the self beyond the limits of nature, even infinitely beyond" (47).

Boyle waxes sentimental in his effort to plumb the depths of Joyce's conflict-ridden Catholicism and frequently gets carried away by his own religious enthusiasms. His presentation is an inspired one, if sometimes overly subjective, overstated, and undersupported. At the heart of his analysis, too, we find a desire to separate the author from Stephen Dedalus and to preserve the former's religious integrity. The crucial lesson that Joyce had learned by *Finnegans Wake* Stephen would never learn: it is, simply, love, or in the words of May Dedalus, "what the heart is, and how it feels." Joyce understood the most profound expression of that sentiment to be a religious one, and, following the example of another Jesuit, Gerald Manley Hopkins, "allow[ed] himself to acknowledge some aspects of Hopkins's positive and profound expression of Jesuit love" (79).

Boyle's efforts to redeem Joyce's reputation, to sanctify the artist who had been damned by others, gain support from other Catholic readers who admired Joyce. Our survey would not be complete without a brief consideration of L. A. G. Strong's contribution to this exculpatory effort, *The Sacred River* (1958). Strong notes the irony that Joyce was branded as atheistic and licentious when, in fact, his life was marked by discipline and austerity and his work showed his dedication to religious principles. Strong terms *Ulysses* "a great Catholic novel" (79); "*Finnegans Wake* could only have been written by a man whose whole attitude to life and to his art was religious" (11). "[Joyce] led a dedicated life: and those who would condemn him need to be very sure that their own faith is as clear, and their integrity as strong" (161).

Strong portrays Joyce as a heroic teller-of-truths, a profoundly religious individual who would not be satisfied with the dogmatism and prudery of the Church. Joyce's work probed the depths of the human mind relentlessly and without inhibition. Joyce was the modern-day Dante, descending into the inferno of contemporary civilization to integrate the fractured modern psyche and redeem a fallen humanity. Strong applauds Joyce's courage and faith:

[Joyce] would attempt for himself what the Church had not done for him: more than that, something which in his judgment the Church had failed to do. He would redeem the Dragon. He would go down into hell, in the steps of Odysseus, Dante, and Swift. From its depths, accepting life's deepest pain, he would raise a triumphant cry, as Shakespeare did in *Lear* and *Hamlet* and *Macbeth*. . . . He would make a ladder joining hell to heaven, after Blake, and with Blake link religion with the feminine principle in life. Inspired by the Romantics, he would open wide the gate between conscious and unconscious, shadow and light. Side by side with the prophets of his own time, he would make friends with the shadow, look on the great archetypes, face his own darkness, and redeem it. (161)

Strong's Joyce is a romantic hero and cult leader, somewhat akin to Kristian Smidt's Blakean mystic. He heralds the return of the repressed and declares nothing in the range of human thought and behavior to be outside the bounds of holiness. He is anything but Kenner's detached ironist. It is not surprising to discover that unlike Kenner, Strong celebrates the affirmation in Molly's final "Yes": "That 'yes,' that fundamental and final acceptance of the human situation, is Joyce's cry of faith. It is made in terms of his feminine side, his inferior function, his feeling" (154).

Hugh Kenner may have unwittingly provided the proper subtitle for this survey of Catholic commentary on Joyce with the title of his 1978 study, *Joyce's Voices*. As some Catholic critics have suggested, Joyce was haunted by voices from his past—from religious authorities, from his own priestly superego—that he could not expunge from his fiction. But "Joyce's Voices" is apropos here for other reasons, too. Joyce spoke in many voices in his fiction. He owned multiple and sometimes contradictory points of view, and not only on the subject of Catholicism. The difficulty any critic faces in assessing Joyce's perspective is in determining which of Joyce's voices he will listen to. One may hear a clear, evenly pitched tenor, a screech, a titter, or a howl; orchestral harmony or a cacophony of discrete and meaningless noises. As we have seen, the critic who bends his ear to Joyce's fiction frequently hears the sound that pleases him or that corroborates his own moral or aesthetic views. This is often the music that the critic himself might have performed had he been in possession of Joyce's instruments.

   Although there exists the danger of oversimplification when approaching Joyce's work from a theological, theoretical, or ideological position, a more circumspect criticism ought to militate against this very tendency. The value of these approaches lies in the discovery of unnoticed elements or veiled tendencies that enlarge the scope of a writer's achievement. For example, the assertion made by all of the critics examined in this chapter—that Joyce possessed deep religious convictions—is itself a challenge to the point of view of those such as Paul Elmer More, who regarded Joyce's work as blasphemy. In more general terms, commentary such as that of Morse, Smidt, Noon, and Strong reminds us that Joyce's sensibility was a complicated and ambivalent one, affected in more ways than we are aware by a Catholic upbringing and worldview. Although we may dispute the particulars of their portraits and object to their some-times too-enthusiastic embrace of Joyce as a fellow-believer, their contribution lies in their elaboration of the portrait of our artist. Joyce becomes not a proud, self-indulgent aesthete but a humble seeker of communion; not a naturalist absorbed in the "time-flux" but a mystic seeking transcendence; not a pornographer or a nihilist but a modern St. Francis who confers his blessing on all things human; not an atheist but a believer; not a mocker, but a redeemer of his fellows. The portrayal of Joyce as a Catholic, rendered to a large degree by Catholics, affirms at the very least that a moral sensibility and moral vision underlie Joyce's work.

Much of the commentary by Catholic critics that fol-lowed the publication of Kenner's *Dublin's Joyce* may be viewed as a response to that book. Wittingly or unwit-tingly, Morse, Noon, Boyle, Smidt, and Strong all qual-ify and temper Kenner's portrait of Joyce, redrawing it with softer contours. Their Joyce is not so dour or so severely judgmental as Kenner's. He is both critical and conciliatory, rather than angry and stern; compassionate and sentimental, rather than detached and ironic; affirma-tive and visionary, rather than skeptical or even cynical. The religious temperament they attributed to Joyce lacked the mean and reactionary character of Kenner's and, to some degree, Eliot's imagining. In addition, this Joyce lacked "orthodoxy" or conventionality in his religious beliefs, and was applauded, by Smidt and Strong in particular, for his efforts to fashion a counterreligion in his art. Theirs is a portrait of the artist as a religious romantic, one fallen victim to the disease that Eliot and Kenner might describe as Stephen-itis.

Although it may not be inevitable, theology may lead to gross distortion or simplification of Joyce's art. As much as the portraits we have examined may differ or resemble one another, we often sense gaps, omissions, and misrepresentations in all these responses. Joyce's humor, Joyce's obscenity, and Joyce's irrepressible irony are too frequently ignored or softpedalled by Catholic readers. Perhaps the most obvious omission is this: all of the Catholic critics we have examined, with the possible exception of J. Mitchell Morse, simply do not take Joyce's anti-Catholic pronouncements seriously. When they appear to do so, they insist that while Stephen may have been guilty of blasphemy, Joyce was not. Joyce's antipathy for the Church was at least as deep-seated as his awe of it, and his protest against its repressiveness, its dogmatism, and its authoritarianism was, in his mind, a reasoned and legitimate one. The darker side of Catholicism that Joyce was so familiar with is often effaced from revisionist readings by Catholic intellectuals.

Joyce became to Catholic readers what he had become to political ideologues from both the left and the right: a symbol of things modern. Their repudiation, or even their manipulative embrace of him, was a gesture against the secularism and moral relativism of the modern world, against what Wyndham Lewis called the "surging ecstatic featureless chaos" that described the world as much as it did James Joyce's style. Catholic reclamation projects around Joyce's reputation represent a rejection of much that we associate with the term "modern."

The effort to portray Joyce as a Catholic artist fails finally to show a sufficient understanding of Joyce's temperament and intellectual style. Aside from what he considered to be many other good reasons to leave the Church, Joyce could not accept its doctrinal thinking, and he protected his intellectual independence and creative freedom from it and other "isms" that threatened to usurp them. Though Catholicism may have been in his head, and though socialism may have been in his heart, he was too stubbornly independent, too skeptical, too ambivalent, too estranged, too shamelessly modern—and perhaps, simply too full of the Luciferian pride of soul his detractors accused him of—to associate himself formally with either or to subscribe to their respective sets of beliefs. He would, like Stephen, "fly by those nets," and every critical effort to recapture him, to contain and identify him, falters if it does not acknowledge Joyce's willed and irrevocable exile.

Conclusion:
The Politics of Parallax,
or the Transubstantiation of Joyce's
Political Soul

The question is always arising: What is the real poem? Is it the poem we now perceive? Is it the poem the author consciously intended? Is it the poem the author intended and his first readers read? Well, it is all these things, depending on the state of our knowledge. But in addition the poem is the poem as it has existed in history, as it has lived its life from Then to Now, as it is a thing which submits itself to one kind of perception in one age and another kind of perception in another age, as it exerts in each age a different kind of power. This makes it a thing we can never wholly understand. . . and the mystery, the unreachable part of the poem, is one of its aesthetic elements.

LIONEL TRILLING, 1942

In his introduction to his acclaimed biography of Joyce, Richard Ellmann observes that "few writers have achieved acknowledgment as geniuses and yet aroused so much discontent and reproach as Joyce."

To his Irish countrymen he is still obscene and very likely mad; they were the last of nations to lift the ban on *Ulysses*. To the English he is eccentric and "Irish," an epithet which, considering the variety of the literature produced by Irishmen during the last seventy years, sounds dangerously "English." To the Americans, who have received him most kindly (although he could not bear their country), he is a great experimentalist, a great city man, but possibly too hard of heart; while to the French, among whom Joyce lived for twenty years, he lacks the refined rationalism which would prove him incontestably a man of letters. As a result of these reservations, Joyce holds his place of eminence under fire. (3–4)

Ellmann's gaze extends beyond the temporal and cultural scope of this study, and his conclusion, though sound, may seem understated, given the evidence of early Amer-

171

ican responses presented in the preceding chapters. But Ellmann's statement does remind us that the controversy that greeted Joyce persisted long after his canonization. Joyce does, indeed, "hold his place of eminence under fire," though when Ellmann wrote those words in 1959, the flames had diminished considerably and changed their hue from three decades earlier.

As Ellmann begins to suggest, the nature as well as the intensity of the controversy around Joyce differed according to culture and, we might add, according to the historical moment and the ideological temper of the time. English critics of the 1920s and 1930s objected to Joyce's frank treatment of sexuality (H. G. Wells referred to Joyce's "cloacal obsession" [Deming 1:86]) and to his unflinching examination of the unconscious life of the common man. "Oh, I just can't get over a great, great deal. I can't get over the feeling of wet linoleum and unemptied pails and far worse horrors in the house of his mind— he's so terribly *unfein*," lamented Katherine Mansfield, with genteel disdain (quoted in Deming 1:22). *Ulysses*, wrote Virginia Woolf in her private diary, was "an illiterate, underbred book . . . the book of a self taught working man" (*Diary* 22). Although she later conceded that, "difficult or unpleasant as we may judge it, [*Ulysses*] is undeniably important" (*Common Reader* 190–1), she still faulted it for its narrow scope, its solipsism, and its indecency. F. R. Leavis omitted Joyce from the canon of great English writers in *The Great Tradition* in 1948, only confirming the marginalization Joyce had long suffered even outside the Bloomsbury circle. Leavis agreed with D. H. Lawrence, who castigated Joyce for "a desire to 'do dirt' on life" in *Ulysses* (Leavis 26). Irish criticism of Joyce focused, not surprisingly, on the unflattering portraits Joyce presented of the Irish people and the Catholic church.

Many Irish caricatured Joyce as a pornographer and as an irrepressible jokester and punster whose works contained little of serious import. If, on the publication of the German translation in 1928, Ernst Robert Curtius called *Ulysses* "one of the most important spiritual events of our time" (Deming 2:451), it was hardly a salutary one: "Joyce's work comes from the revolt of the spirit and leads to the destruction of the world. . . . A metaphysical nihilism is the substance of Joyce's work" (Deming 2:469).

The controversy *Ulysses* generated in American literary circles sprang more directly from political polarization and moral prudery than from class snobbery. The novel underwent a most interesting latency period in America during the twenties and thirties when, in all its rawness and daring and mystery, it became an issue in the broader debate over the moral and political responsibility of the artist. Polemics dominated literary discussions. Ironically, denunciations of "bourgeois" modernist art from the left sounded remarkably similar in tone as well as phrasing to the attacks on "irresponsible" artists emanating from the right. The artistic priorities announced by the social realists early in the 1930s influenced fellow travelers as well as more independent-minded American Marxists: "proletarian" art would be celebrated over "bourgeois," "content" would be privileged over "form," "clarity" would displace "obscurity," faith in class solidarity would triumph over solipsism and despair. New Humanists and antifascist liberals called for a renewed moral and political commitment in literature, an invigorated sense of "responsibility" that would mobilize the American public against the threat of fascism overseas and would retard or reverse the process of domestic social change. Faced with the crises of contemporary life so distressingly evoked in *Ulysses* and other modern art, the right responded with an idealized vision of the past, while the left looked eagerly toward an imagined future.

Underlying the American debate over the meaning and value of *Ulysses* was an evolving discussion about the function of culture and the role of criticism. Set against the narrow and self-serving definitions proffered by New Humanists or by Stalinist ideologues, Edmund Wilson, Philip Rahv, Lionel Trilling, and others sympathetic to Marxism in the late 1930s offered a more ample and encompassing notion of culture that could embrace a work of genius like *Ulysses* without abandoning an expectation that art should serve some moral purpose. They defended the autonomy of art from politics and sought to preserve what Trilling would call the "variousness and possibility" so vital to a dynamic cultural life. From the vantage point of 1946, with the lessons of the previous decade clearly in mind, Trilling would appeal for the subordination of politics to art: "Unless we insist that politics is imagination and mind, we will learn that imagination and mind are politics, and of a kind that we will not like" (quoted in Chace, *Lionel Trilling* 17–18).

Trilling recognized that what lured the American critic and writer into political activity was what Phillip Rahv had called in 1939 a "frustrated social impulse" ("Proletarian Literature" 298). American writers had long been engaged in the ritual of self-justification before a skeptical and pragmatic reading public (even, too, before their own expatriate literary brethren who, like Henry James, found American social life too stunted for the possibilities of their own fiction). The crises of the twenties and thirties presented American artists and intellectuals with what they perceived to be a long-denied opportunity to assume social and political leadership. Their excesses in this direction must be understood as both a pent-up expression of their idealism and a naive overestimation of their own potential power. Irving Howe points out that modern American criticism has often served as "a surrogate mode of speech for people blocked in public life." "Unable to fulfill directly their visions of politics, morality, and religion, critics transfer these to the seemingly narrower channels of literary criticism. Precisely this spilling over of thought and passion has made criticism so interesting in our time—so perilous, too" (*Margin* 147).

Largely due to the efforts of Edmund Wilson, what did survive from the debate over *Ulysses* in the 1930s was a characterization of Joyce as a shrewd but comprehensible innovator whose insights into individual consciousness did not defame humanity but ennobled it. Wilson proclaimed that with *Ulysses*, "Joyce . . . brought into literature a new and unknown beauty"; Joyce was no less than the "poet of . . . the new self-consciousness of the modern world" (*Axel's Castle* 220–21). In his praise of *Ulysses*, Wilson challenged caricatures of Joyce as a prig or misanthrope. In the trajectory of Joyce criticism beyond the 1930s, Wilson's contribution was most important, for it established Joyce as a skilled but not heartless technician; as a fastidious recorder of the details of urban life and a prober of the secrets of the unconscious mind; and most importantly, as a liberal who advanced progressive human values. Joyce's political consciousness would be continually studied and diagnosed, with other readers reaching conclusions at variance with Wilson's. But Wilson was the catalyst in the launching of Joyce's reputation as what we might call a "good" liberal, a characterization that would be reinforced and amplified by James T. Farrell, Trilling, Howe, Harry Levin, Delmore Schwartz, and most exhaustively, by Richard Ellmann.

Counterreadings of Joyce's political soul were advanced by critics from both the left and the right, some
denouncing the liberalism that others celebrated, some
applauding a reactionary sensibility that others reviled.
Wyndham Lewis excoriated Joyce in his 1927 essay, "An
Analysis of the Mind of James Joyce." Whereas Wilson
praised Joyce's pioneering exploration of human consciousness, Lewis condemned *Ulysses* "for its emphasis
upon . . . the self-conscious time sense," a defect he
ascribed variously and vaguely to the influence of Berg-
son, Einstein, and Freud (92). Whereas Wilson praised
Joyce because his "grasp on his objective world never
slips" ("We possess Dublin, seen, heard, smelt and felt"
[39]), Lewis complained of the plethora of detail in
Ulysses, which created "a certain deadness, a lack of . . .
animal vigour" in the text. And while Wilson hailed the
reconciliation of Molly and Leopold Bloom in *Ulysses*
as the "greatest moral climax of the story" (*Axel's Castle*
224), Lewis asserted that *Ulysses* suffered from "an absence of meaning, an emptiness of philosophic content,
a poverty of new and disturbing observation" (102).
Lewis's aristocratic values and classical tastes in art man-
ifested themselves again and again in his critique of Joyce,
whom he mocked as the "poet of the shabby-genteel, im-
poverished intellectualism of Dublin" (125). "Joyce is like
an over-mellow hot-house pear, with an attractive musi-
cal delivery," wrote Lewis elsewhere (quoted in Meyers
140). *Ulysses* mirrored the changes in the modern world
Lewis deplored; it was an emblem of the "surging ecstatic
featureless chaos set up as an ideal, in place of the noble
exactitude of harmonious proportion of the European
scientific ideal—the specifically Western heaven" (129).
Lewis was an unabashed reactionary who regarded Joyce

as a passionless technician, an equivocating and tiresome documentarian of the decadence of contemporary life.

Others who shared Lewis's conservative politics, such as T. S. Eliot, would reach different conclusions about Joyce and find in him an ideological ally. Eliot's brief but influential essay, "*Ulysses*, Order, and Myth," was the first significant contribution to a strain of Joyce criticism that tended to portray the artist as a reactionary. Ironically, some critics on the left would also identify Joyce as a reactionary. But while Stalinist ideologues would characterize Joyce as a "bad" reactionary, a decadent bourgeois ("Joyceism is a most reactionary philosophy of social pessimism, misanthropy, barrenness and doom," wrote R. Miller-Budnitskaya in 1938), Eliot celebrated Joyce as an artist whose method made "the modern world possible for art." The insinuation that Joyce was a "good" reactionary would gain its fullest and most overt expression in the early work of Hugh Kenner, particularly in *Dublin's Joyce*, published in 1956. Kenner found fault with Lewis's reading of *Ulysses*, though he was ambivalent enough to declare it "the most brilliant misreading in modern criticism" (362). According to Kenner, Lewis's polemicism had blinded him to the subtle manner in which Joyce delivered his indictment of the wasteland of modern life. Kenner read a parodic intent in Joyce's use of the details of modern urban life and the clichéd characters and voices that filled *Ulysses*. And Kenner took pains to disassociate Joyce from his artistic alter-ego, Stephen Dedalus, whom he claimed Joyce relentlessly lampooned. In so doing, Kenner sired what one critic has called "the Stephen-hating school" of Joyce criticism, in which a significant number of Joyce's Catholic readers would enroll.

In "*Ulysses*: Joyce's Intentions," a polemic included in

his 1984 collection of essays, *Using Biography*, William
Empson attacked Kenner's portrayal of Joyce as a satirist
and parodist who adopted a uniformly ironic tone toward
his characters, particularly toward Stephen Dedalus. Con-
fronting what he called "the Kenner Smear," Empson rejected Kenner's characterization of Stephen as an artistic
buffoon and argued instead that Stephen's artistic ambitions and moral claim be taken seriously. Kenner,
claimed Empson, was simply wrong to view Stephen not
as the young James Joyce but "as a possible fatal alternative, a young man who has taken some wrong turn or
slipped over the edge of some vast drop, so that he can
never grow into the wise old author (intensely Christian,
though in a mystically paradoxical way) who writes the
book" (Empson 204). Empson allowed that we are meant
to laugh at both Bloom and Stephen but not in the deri-
sive way Kenner would have us, not "as the Blessed in
the Christian Heaven. . . enjoy their eternal ringside view
of the torments of Hell" (209). Drawing on Ellmann's
biography of Joyce and Joyce's published letters—"using
biography," as the title of his book promised—Empson
argued that Joyce was relentlessly and insistently anti-
Catholic and was more in sympathy with his characters
than Kenner claimed. Empson found a moral rather than
a moralizing tone in *Ulysses*: the moral force of *Ulysses* lay
in the union of the artist and the citizen and the possibility of a triangular relationship involving Molly.

   Empson's heated rebuttal of Kenner's reading of Joyce
dramatizes for us the schism that has developed in modern Joyce criticism, whose fault lines, I would argue, lie
in the debates over the Joycean weltanschauung dating
from the 1920s and 1930s. Empson wished to reconstitute
Joyce as the controversial figure he in fact was in life.
("Joyce did not have to complain of being thought a

Christian. . . till he was dead," noted Empson [215].)
But he also wished to restore to the portrait of our artist a
sense of his geniality and humor and an appreciation of
the moral impulses that drove his art. In this respect,
Empson joins that collection of American Joyce critics,
for whom Edmund Wilson was mentor, who shared the
belief that Joyce's work was anchored in affirmative
moral values.

More than any modern Joyce critic, Richard Ellmann
has advanced Joyce's reputation as a political liberal and
has stood for the last three decades as Kenner's principal
adversary. In both his biography of Joyce, first published
in 1959, and especially in *The Consciousness of Joyce*
(1977), Ellmann has elaborated a portrait of Joyce as an
artist who relentlessly challenged the authority of Church
and State and who was ever mindful of the moral force of
his work. Though he may be rightly accused of indirect-
ness ("obliquity" is the term Ellmann prefers), "one always knows where Joyce is, even though he never says"
(*Consciousness* 73–74). "Joyce," adds Ellmann, "was more
radical than Homer or Shakespeare, the least willing to
accept the world as he found it" (76). Ellmann insists that
Joyce's art is implicitly aligned with socialistic and democratic political values, that it affirms the spirit and recog-
nizes the "communal role of art" (74), and that it appeals
for the unity of humankind while acknowledging its
diversity.

We might dramatize the differences between Ellmann's
and Kenner's reading of Joyce by briefly examining their
responses to Bloom, that "first great hero of unheroic
literature" (Cronin 97). Bloom was Joyce's bold master-
stroke, at once both mediocre and majestic, banal and
profound, ridiculous yet sublimely good. He represented,
above all else, Joyce's rebuke to the anti-Semitism so

fashionable among the literati of his time. The symbol of deracinated modern man, Bloom served as the meandering and inarticulate carrier of the undisplayed banner of Joyce's pacifism, his humanitarianism, and his democratic liberalism.

For the Kenner writing *Dublin's Joyce*, Bloom, the "timid cuckold" (356), was something less than heroic. Bloom was an evocation of the debased world from which he sprang. Kenner warned us that we ought not to sentimentalize Bloom or regard him as anything more than another member of the living dead: "Bloom is not entitled to sentimental regard as the champion of the plain man. He is the most inadequate Messiah imaginable" (256). In Kenner's view, Joyce's novel takes us on a Dantean descent into hell, into a modern "inferno whose apotheosis is the debris-crammed brain of hapless Leopold Bloom" (230).

Ellmann offers us a strikingly different perspective on Bloom. Ellmann argues in *The Consciousness of Joyce* that Joyce's intention in *Ulysses* was to unite Stephen and Bloom "by displaying their underlying agreement on political views which the author thereby underwrites" (90). Although neither Stephen nor Bloom offers a coherent program of political change, each affirms an indistinct set of political values in the act of criticizing the inadequacies of Irish secular and religious life. Stephen affirms "the disused possibilities of life," prodding his countrymen to jettison the "petrified dogmas" by which they live. Bloom's kindness and goodwill translate into a credo of love, "a crude term for his sense of mutuality of concern but at least a traditional one" (85). Joyce's own sympathy for the Irish nationalist movement and his particular admiration for its leader, Arthur Griffith, were expressed through Bloom, who, Molly worries in her soliloquy, courts danger through his association with Griffith and Sinn Fein. Bloom, "the most inadequate Messiah imaginable" according to Kenner, assumes quite a different posture in Ellmann's reading of *Ulysses*:

Unimpressive as Bloom may seem in so many ways, unworthy to catch marlin or countesses with Hemingway's characters, or to sop up guilt with Faulkner's, or to sit on committees with C. P. Snow's, Bloom is a humble vessel elected to bear and transmit unimpeached the best qualities of the mind. Joyce's discovery, so humanistic that he would have been embarrassed to disclose it out of context, was that the ordinary is the extraordinary. (*James Joyce* 5)

Using Bloom as his touchstone, Ellmann constructs a portrait of Joyce as more forgiving than censorious, more benevolent than vindictive, and more inclusive in his reach than exclusionary. One need not strain to hear in Ellmann's words the echoes of Edmund Wilson's appraisal of Joyce's principal characters, written three decades earlier:

Stephen, Bloom and Mrs. Bloom are certainly not either unamiable or unattractive—and for all their misfortunes and shortcomings, they inspire us with considerable respect. (219)

Bloom . . . has the strength of humility. . . . [He] is all the possibilities of that ordinary humanity which is somehow not so ordinary after all. (*James Joyce* 223)

Robert Scholes, in his recent essay, "Joyce and Modernist Ideology," faults Ellmann for tempering Joyce's political views and not taking seriously enough Joyce's commitment to socialism. Ellmann's former student, Dominic Manganiello, documents in *Joyce's Politics* Joyce's early interest in anarchism and socialism. During

1906–1907, says Scholes, "Joyce thought of himself—frequently and earnestly—as a socialist" (96). Scholes describes the young James Joyce as "antibourgeois, anticlerical, antiparliamentary, antimilitaristic, antibureaucratic, an Irish nationalist, and definitely not an anti-Semite" (102). After 1907, Joyce "certainly took less interest in politics, but he neither repudiated his earlier views nor adopted any of the alternatives that were so visible and insistent around him" (96). Scholes situates Joyce among the ideological currents of his time and notes that the political idealism that spurred him early in his career did not evolve into the authoritarianism of Mussolini's Fascism or the dogmatism of Lukacs's Marxism. Scholes points out that the consciousness of each of these three epochal figures in early twentieth-century politics and art was forged by similar cultural pressures which resulted in striking resemblances in their early histories and political orientations. Although Joyce's artistic ambitions overtook his political radicalism, Scholes argues, they never extinguished it. As an artist, Joyce was poised between the naturalism and aestheticism that represented the polar tendencies of modernist art. He would not yield to the fragmentation, says Scholes, "need[ing] to reconcile the naturalistic presentation of life with an aesthetic control that would affect the personal conscience" (103). Here again, we are reminded of Edmund Wilson's praise of *Ulysses*: "[Joyce] has, in *Ulysses*, exploited together, as no writer had thought to do before, the resources of both Symbolism and Naturalism" (*Axel's Castle* 204).

Scholes and Manganiello extend and further document Ellmann's assertions about Joyce's early political activities and the direction of his political consciousness. G. J. Watson, in "The Politics of *Ulysses*," addresses more directly the content of *Ulysses* as he builds a case for Joyce's political radicalism. Watson takes issue with the notion that *Ulysses* is either apolitical or reactionary in character. The particular target of Watson's polemic is Phillip Herring, who in his essay "Joyce's Politics" advances a view of Joyce as an unfeeling, self-serving neurotic whose politics would most accurately be described as reactionary. Watson is largely in agreement with Dominic Manganiello's conclusions about Joyce, though he faults Manganiello for failing to draw adequately the connection between Joyce's politics and his aesthetics. Moreover, according to Watson, this connection is a more profound and obvious one than poststructuralists such as Colin MacCabe have argued. Joyce's radicalism goes beyond "refus[ing] a hierarchy of discourses within the text," as MacCabe asserts. "The politics of Joyce's *Ulysses*," writes Watson, "may be seen as a characteristically massive attempt to deconstruct the mythology of Romantic Ireland" (41). Placing *Ulysses* within an Irish political and cultural context in which he argues it must be understood, Watson iterates throughout his essay the specifically Irish targets of Joyce's assault:

The cult of the peasant and a corresponding hatred of the commercial and urban; an exclusivist sense of the nature of "true" Irishness; a belief in the dynamic power of myth, that "great legends are the mothers of great nations"; a deeply atavistic faith in blood sacrifice; and an attitude toward history which is simultaneously aesthetic and theatrical, teleological and even apocalyptic. . . . It is the systematic and comprehensive thoroughness with which *Ulysses* confronts and affronts the pieties of . . . romantic nationalism that enforces our sense of the work as vigorously political. (41–42)

Watson builds a convincing case for reading *Ulysses* as
"vigorously political." Although Joyce, unlike Yeats,
eschewed political theorizing, it is enough that he fulfilled
Chekhov's injunction to the artist to accurately present
the problem. "Joyce the skeptic moves among the ideal-
ists of the time with his sane detachment," notes Watson;
he confronts in *Ulysses* both "the rhetorician and the
sentimentalist with a vision of reality honest, truthful,
sane—and humorous" (56).

Watson joins Scholes, Ellmann, Manganiello, and
Richard Brown in reminding us how implicated Joyce's
life and work were in the political movements and issues
of his day. "In spite of Joyce's reputation of having
skirted his age, he is unexpectedly at its center" writes
Ellmann, (*James Joyce* 4). If Joyce was indeed at the "center" of his age, his work posed an unrelenting challenge
to its institutions, its traditions, and its beliefs. It is not
difficult to see why Joyce failed to please those readers
who approached him with a vested interest in what he
dared to question or defile. But as for those critics on the
left who might otherwise have been sympathetic to
Joyce's egalitarian sentiments and oppositionalist posture,
we must look beyond their frequent tirades against
Joyce's obscurity and elitism to explain their displeasure.
We might simply dismiss the early Marxist responses to
Ulysses in the 1930s as crude expressions of ideological
groupthink if we did not see vestiges of them in subsequent Marxist readings, particularly those of Georg
Lukacs and his student, Peter Egri. Surely the Stalinists
were too eagerly erecting barriers between bourgeois
reactionaries and socialist realists. Nevertheless, they
were correct to identify a sensibility different from their
own expressing itself in the pages of *Ulysses*, one that did
not endorse their conception of the march of history or

their faith in the emergence of a new man. Lukacs echoed earlier Marxists' dissatisfaction with Joyce when he criticized *Ulysses* for its stylistic excesses, its preoccupation with individual consciousness, and its relative poverty of ideas. But Lukacs objected more generally to the allegorizing tendencies of modernist writers ("Every person, every object, every relationship can stand for something else" [Scholes 106]), an objection which Robert Scholes suggests is at the heart of his disappointment with Joyce: "It is surely [the allegorical tendencies of modernism] and the Joycean sense that history is an endless repetition of such transformations that make Joyce a fearful object to Lukacs, whose faith in progressive possibilities could only abhor what he called the 'religious atheism' that animated Joyce's modernism" (106).

Of course, apropos of the duplexity so integral to the Joycean universe, one person's regress is another's progress. Richard Ellmann, who refers to Joyce's allegorizing technique as a "series of doublings and undoublings" (*Consciousness* 94), argues that this results not in a suffocating sense of nihilism or despair but in a recognition of "fertile," if limited, human possibility.

With this recognition of universal intermingling Joyce attained his final unstated statement about life. . . . What he had discovered was not that all forms were one form—a mystical conclusion—but rather that all forms proceed by incessant doublings and undoublings in which they remain enantiomorphous—that is, resembling each other but not superposable. Hierarchies disappear and the "aristocracies are supplanted," for all elements are common elements. (*Consciousness* 95)

Joyce was not a sentimentalist, Ellmann reminds us, either in his view of human nature or of the possibilities

presented by political reform. "I distrust all enthusiasms,"
he had once said, and whatever sense of hope or affirmation appears in his work is always circumscribed by caution, ambivalence, and the laughter born of reversals and
contradictions.

The controversy over Joyce among Marxists is just one
illustration of the breach between Joyce and the political
zeitgeist of his time. Set against a host of orthodoxies,
moderating against a current of extremism, remaining
left while his modernist contemporaries moved decidedly
right, Joyce declared insistently his intellectual independence. He would serve no ideological master—not religious, not political, not artistic. Nothing escaped the
reach of his irony, least of all the image of himself
satirized in the figure of Stephen Dedalus and Shem the
Penman. He was bound to disappoint an audience of contemporaries who looked urgently toward art to confirm a
vision of a world that his work declared no longer existed
or would not likely come into being. Edmund Wilson
heralded Joyce as "the great poet of a new phase of the
human consciousness" (221), a phase which, he might
have added, Joyce's audience was unready to welcome or
adopt. The ontological and epistemological challenges at
the center of Joyce's work required not only a new artistic form but a new reader as well. The multiplicity of
perspectives he offered, his allusiveness of style, his fragmentation of consciousness, his relativistic notion of
truth—these were the cornerstones of Joyce's work,
which begged for a reader as prescient, as balanced, as
nuanced—and as rare—as Wilson himself.

The reader Joyce required was the reader his work
labored to create. Stephen sets forth at the end of *Portrait*
to "forge in the smithy of my soul the uncreated conscience of my race." Lofty and perhaps laughable as that

aspiration might appear when we confront him at the opening of *Ulysses*, it was not a sentiment Joyce himself ever abandoned. His method would not, of course, be exhortation, but indirection, reticence, subtlety; silence, exile, and particularly cunning would be his modus operandi. Joyce joked that he sought "the ideal reader with the ideal insomnia," but what beyond the boredom or compulsiveness implied in that comment did Joyce ask from his readers? Patience, humility, compassion, moral and intellectual courage, a tolerance for ambiguity, a willingness to laugh at grave matters.

[Joyce] denudes man of what we are accustomed to respect, then summons us to sympathize. For Joyce, as for Socrates, understanding is a struggle, best when humiliating. We can move closer to him by climbing over the obstacles of our pretensions, but as we do so he tasks our prowess again by his difficult language. He requires that we adapt ourselves in form as well as in content to his new point of view. (Ellmann, *James Joyce* 6)

"Joyce was no closet novelist," adds Ellmann in *The Consciousness of Joyce*; "he spoke to the world, confident that one day it would hear him" (9).

The din of cant and dogma may have been too loud for many of his contemporaries to listen well. But Joyce was writing beyond them, not only toward an ideal reader but toward a culture less encumbered by custom, prejudice, or ideology, one large and various and tolerant enough to appreciate his achievement. America would eventually provide Joyce with his most substantial reading audience, though his canonization would not begin to occur until the ascendancy of the New Critics in the 1940s and 1950s. *Ulysses* would endure the controversies of the 1920s and 1930s before it began to receive the studied attention it had always demanded. But while the New Critics rescued *Ulysses* from the cultural trench warfare of preceding decades, they exhibited their own shortcomings as readers, replacing one form of narrowness with another. In their fetishizing of literary form, they missed much of the book's bawdiness and humor and gave scant consideration to the political substrata of the novel. *Ulysses*, however, would survive even its own canonization. Subsequent readers, some of whom I have surveyed here, would restore to it those elements that were downplayed or effaced by critics eager to appropriate it for their particular purposes.

The history of Joyce's reception in America makes us keenly aware of how political and ideological pressures have retarded and advanced his reputation. But this history also reminds us how a genius of Joyce's caliber, and how a book as grand and elusive as *Ulysses*, outlasts, if not transcends, those pressures. *Ulysses* exerts over time an ineluctable pressure of its own upon the culture that receives it, finally subsuming appropriative efforts, extending the capacities of its readers, and altering the cultural landscape in unexpected ways. The final and most profound of the many challenges *Ulysses* offers is to its individual and collective audience to be equal to the task of reading it. And in our effort to accommodate ourselves to this unaccommodating book, we are humbled, and perhaps enlarged. In the letter and spirit of Joycean paradox, "the longest way round is the shortest way home." We are, indeed, in the fullest sense of Richard Ellmann's words, "still learning to be Joyce's contemporaries" (*James Joyce* 3).

Notes

Introduction

1. In conversation, Eliot did express private doubts about some aspects of *Ulysses*. Richard Ellmann quotes Virginia Woolf's description in her diary of Eliot as "rapt, enthusiastic" about *Ulysses* in a discussion they had just after its publication. "Yet," Ellmann continues, "the book gave no new insight into human nature such as *War and Peace* did, Eliot granted, and added, 'Bloom tells one nothing. Indeed, this new method of giving the psychology proves to my mind that it doesn't work. It doesn't tell as much as some casual glance from outside often does'" (*James Joyce* 528).

Chapter 1

1. Cowley's remark deserves some qualification. Some distinguished work was produced by writers who, however briefly, aligned themselves with the Party. Richard Wright's *Native Son* and Henry Roth's *Call It Sleep* are two examples.

2. The passage reads in full: "[Joyce's] whole world lies between a cupboardful of medieval books, a brothel and a pothouse. For him, the national revolutionary movement of the Irish petty bourgeoisie does not exist; and consequently, the picture which he presents, despite its ostensible impartiality, is untrue."

3. In "What the Revolutionary Movement Can Do For a Writer" (90), Cowley cites Joyce's *Portrait* as exemplary of a host of books whose concern is the conflict between the individual and society. Cowley criticized the tendency to concentrate on the artist's consciousness and neglect "society, the outer world."

Chapter 2

1. While Joyce dismissed Lawrence's work as "propaganda," Lawrence reportedly complained to his wife that the last part of *Ulysses* was "the dirtiest, most obscene thing ever written. . . . It is filthy "(quoted in Ellmann, *James Joyce* 628). Pound had misgivings about *Finnegans Wake* during its serial publication in the 1930s, though he maintained respect for Joyce. In an essay published in 1933, Pound complained that

I can not see that Mr. Joyce's later work concerns more than a few specialists, and I can not see in it either a comprehension of, or a very great preoccupation with, the present, which may indicate an obtuseness on my part, or may indicate that Mr. Joyce's present and my present are very different one from the other, and, further, that I can not believe in a passive acceptance. (Read, *Pound/ Joyce* 251)

2. Edmund Wilson's "Archibald MacLeish and 'the Word,'" a rejoinder to MacLeish's essay, is an example of just such an effective rebuttal.

3. MacLeish's omission of Joyce in his general indictment of the modernists may owe to his early personal acquaintance with Joyce in the 1920s, when MacLeish himself was an expatriate and an aspiring poet. He expressed both fondness and admiration for Joyce in his correspondence, first in a fawning, half-articulate letter to the older author written several days after hearing him read from *Work in Progress* (in Paris, 1927); and second, in a 1954 letter to Richard Ellmann, in which he expressed some of the awe he seemed always to have felt for Joyce. Though the letters (excerpts printed below) were written before and after the period of MacLeish's political activism, they may indicate why he refrained from criticizing Joyce during that period.

Dear Mr. Joyce:
I had not yesterday—nor have I today for that matter—words to tell you how the pages you read us moved and excited me. This pure creation that goes almost beyond the power of the words you use is something I cannot talk about. But neither can I keep silence. This I am sure—that what you have done is something even you can be proud to have written.

                                                            Faithfully yours,

                                                            Archibald MacLeish

[To Richard Ellmann:]
. . . But then I never found Joyce warm. I liked him. The little beard. The thick
lenses. Like a very professional doctor—not a practicing one but a man about a
hospital, rarely seen. I liked his shyness and his stiffness and the sense of something vivid and maybe dangerous under it. I don't know what "greatness" in a
man is though I think I know that it is in a man's work. But a great *man*! . . .
But in Joyce you felt a hard, strong actuality that, if not greatness, was at least
something you were always conscious of.
(*James Joyce* 598)

4. Wilson confided in a 1957 letter to Brooks that he had been
"brooding on Eliot since our conversation" and had concluded that
Eliot was both "scoundrel and actor":

The shrewd Yankee operator who always remains discreet but gets away with
murder is balanced by the Yankee idealist who—in literature, the only thing
about which he feels intensely—is able to stand by his convictions and, on
occasion, without sticking his neck out (as Lewis and Pound habitually did), to
show a firm courage. In his tiresome performances as the humble great man, he
is more and more betraying his vanity: he talks about his own work in far too
many of this last collection of essays. He is absurd in his pretensions to ponti-
ficate. . . . But I know that you regard him as a more sinister figure. (*Letters*
549)

Chapter 3

1. Farrell seemed to have a particularly contentious relationship
with Eastman, whom he accused in "Literature and Ideology" of having paved the way for Brooks et al. with his attacks on the modernists
in "The Cult of Unintelligibility." Eastman, a lapsed Marxist as well
as a lapsed Stalinist, responded by urging Farrell to break from "the
nearsighted cranks and cross patchers, the wounded veterans of an exploded theology" and build "a new radical movement. . . based on a
straightout recognition that Marxism is unscientific and complete col-
lectivism a failure" ("Values and Facts" 207).
2. Irving Howe, *A Margin of Hope*, 56. Here is the context of
Howe's reference to Wilson:

At the age of sixteen I was lent a copy of Edmund Wilson's *Axel's Castle* by a
YPSL friend in the Bronx. This was probably the first book of literary criticism
I read through from start to finish, even though I had only a skimpy acquain-
tance with the writers Wilson discussed. Something about Wilson's moral

gravity moved me. It always would, though in 1936 I could not yet know I
had encountered one of the figures I would come to regard as an intellectual
model.

Chapter 4

1. Ransom, "Reconstructed But Unregenerate," 14. Ransom used
the term to contrast Southern with English aristocracy and with
Graeco-Roman civilization. Here is the context of his reference:
"Southern society was not an institution of very showy elegance, for
the so-called aristocrats were mostly home-made and countrified.
Aristocracy is not the word which defines this social organization so
well as squirearchy, which I borrow from a recent article by Mr. William Frierson in the *Sewanee Review*."

2. See Van Wyck Brooks, *The Opinions of Oliver Allston* (1941),
199, 255–26, 228–29, 231; Macdonald, "Kulturbolschewismus Is
Here"; Tate and Ransom, "On the Brooks-MacLeish Thesis," 38–47.

3. Joyce is quoted by Jacques Benoit-Mechin in an interview conducted by Richard Ellmann in 1956 (*James Joyce* 535).

Chapter 5

1. Eliot noted in *After Strange Gods* (1933) that the chances for the
reestablishment of a native culture were better in the South. "You are
further from New York City," he told his audience at the University
of Virginia; "you have been less industrialized and less invaded by
foreign races; and you have more opulent soil."

Kenner studied with Brooks at Yale and wrote admiringly of John
Crowe Ransom in "The Pedagogue as Critic."

2. Pound's comment appeared in an essay entitled, "James Joyce et
Pecuchet," *Mercure de France*, 106 (June, 1922), pp. 307–20. A partial
translation appears in Deming, ed., *James Joyce: The Critical Heritage*,
1:263–67.

Here is the context of Pound's remark: "Joyce uses a scaffold taken
from Homer, and the remains of a medieval allegorical culture; it matters little, it is a question of cooking, which does not restrict the
action, nor inconvenience it, nor harm the realism, nor the contemporaneity of the action. It is a means of regulating the form" (264).

3. In *Joyce's Voices*, Kenner would further develop the argument that for Joyce's Irish, reality was constituted of words, and words were of an ever-changing configuration and meaning. There could be no certainties, no absolute meanings in a world so dominated by Pyrrhonism.

4. Kenner referred to Lewis's "An Analysis of the Mind of James Joyce" (1927) as "the most brilliant misreading in modern criticism" (*Dublin's Joyce* 262).

5. It is interesting that Kenner—unlike Eliot and Allen Tate, to name only two examples—responds unsympathetically, even harshly to Gabriel Conroy of "The Dead." Kenner sees no transformation in Gabriel's character at the end of the story, no communal longing, and no possibility for redemption.

6. Both Kevin Sullivan and William T. Noon assert that Kenner errs in reading too much irony into Joyce.

Works Cited

Aaron, Daniel. "Edmund Wilson's Political Decade." In *Literature at the Barricades*, edited by Ralph F. Bogardus and Fred Hobson, 175–86. University, Ala.: The University of Alabama Press, 1982.

———. *Writers on the Left*. New York: Harcourt, Brace and World, 1961.

Adams, R.M. *AfterJoyce*. New York: Oxford University Press, 1977.

Babbitt, Irving. *Rousseau and Romanticism*. Boston: Houghton Mifflin, 1919.

Blackmur, R.P. *Anni Mirabiles, 1921–1925: Reason in the Madness of Letters*. Washington, D.C.: The Library of Congress, 1956.

———. "The Jew in Search of a Son: Joyce's *Ulysses*." In *Eleven Essays in the European Novel*, 27–47. New York: Harcourt, Brace and World, 1943.

Boldereff, Frances M. *Hermes to His Son Thoth: Being Joyce's Use of Giordano Bruno in "Finnegans Wake."* Woodward, Pa.: Classic Nonfiction Library, 1968.

———. *Reading "Finnegans Wake."* Woodward, Pa.: Classic Nonfiction Library, 1959.

Boyle, Robert. S.J. *James Joyce's Pauline Vision: A Catholic Exposition*. Carbondale: Southern Illinois University Press, 1978.

Brooks, Cleanth. *A Shaping Joy: Studies in the Writer's Craft*. London: Methuen, 1971.

Brooks, Van Wyck. *The Opinions of Oliver Allston*. New York: E. P. Dutton, 1941.

Brown, Richard. *James Joyce and Sexuality*. Cambridge: Cambridge University Press, 1985.

Calmer, Alan. "Down with 'Leftism'!" *Partisan Review* 3 (June 1936): 7–9.

Caute, David. *The Fellow-Travellers: A Postscript to the Enlightenment.* New York: Macmillan, 1973.

Chace, William M. *Lionel Trilling: Criticism and Politics.* Stanford: Stanford University Press, 1980.

———. *The Political Identities of Ezra Pound and T. S. Eliot.* Stanford: Stanford University Press, 1973.

———, ed. *Joyce: A Collection of Critical Essays.* Englewood Cliffs, N.J.: Prentice-Hall, Inc., 1974.

Cowley, Malcolm. *The Dream of the Golden Mountains: Remembering the 1930s.* New York: Viking, 1980.

———. *Exile's Return.* 1934. Reprint New York: Penguin, 1976.

———. "Humanizing Society." In Grattan, ed., *The Critique of Humanism*, 63–84.

———. "James Joyce," *Bookman* 59 (July 1924): 518–21.

———. "What the Revolutionary Movement Can Do for a Writer." 1934. Reprinted in *Think Back on Us . . .* , edited by Henry Dan Piper, 87–94. Carbondale: Southern Illinois University Press, 1967.

Cronin, Anthony. "The Advent of Bloom." In Chace, ed., *James Joyce: A Collection of Critical Essays*, 84–101.

Crossman, Richard, ed. *The God that Failed.* New York: Harper and Row, 1950.

Davidson, Donald, et al., *I'll Take My Stand: The South and the Agrarian Tradition.* New York: Harper, 1930. .

Deming, Robert H. *A Bibliography of James Joyce Studies.* Boston: G.K. Hall, 1977.

———, ed. *James Joyce: The Critical Heritage.* 2 vols. New York: Barnes and Noble, 1970.

DeVoto, Bernard. "Exiles from Reality." Review of *Exile's Return*, by Malcolm Cowley. *Saturday Review of Literature* 10 (June 2, 1934): 721–22.

———. *Forays and Rebuttals.* Boston: Little Brown, 1936.

———. *The Literary Fallacy.* Boston: Little Brown, 1944.

Eastman, Max. *Artists in Uniform.* New York: Octagon Books, 1934.

———. "As to Values and Facts: An Exchange." *Partisan Review* 9 (May–June 1942): 203–12.

———. *The Literary Mind.* New York: Charles Scribners, 1931.

Egri, Peter, *Avantgardism and Modernity.* Tulsa: University of Tulsa Press, 1972.

Eliot, T. S. *After Strange Gods: A Primer of Modern Heresy.* London: Faber, 1933.

————. *The Idea of a Christian Society*. 1940. Reprinted in *Christianity and Culture*. New York: Harcourt, Brace, 1960.

————. "A Letter to the Editors." *Partisan Review* 9 (Mar.–Apr. 1942): 115–16.

————."A Message to the Fish." 1941. Reprinted in Givens, ed., *James Joyce: Two Decades of Criticism*, 468–71.

————. *Notes towards the Definition of Culture*. 1949. Reprinted in *Christianity and Culture*.

————. *On Poetry and Poets*. New York: Farrar, Straus, and Cudahy, 1957.

————. "Tradition and the Individual Talent." 1919. Reprinted in *Selected Essays, 1917–1932*, 3–11. New York: Harcourt, Brace, 1932.

————. "*Ulysses*, Order, and Myth." 1923. Reprinted in Givens, ed., *James Joyce: Two Decades of Criticism*, 198–202.

Ellmann, Richard. *The Consciousness of Joyce*. New York: Oxford University Press, 1977.

————. *James Joyce*. New York: Oxford University Press, 1959.

Empson, William. "*Ulysses*: Joyce's Intentions." 1970. Reprinted in *Using Biography*, 203–16. London: Hogarth, 1984.

Farrell, James T. "Joyce's *A Portrait of the Artist as a Young Man*." 1944. Reprinted in *The League of Frightened Philistines*, 45–59.

————. *The League of Frightened Philistines*. New York: Vanguard Press, 1945.

————. "Literature and Ideology." 1942. Reprinted in *The League of Frightened Philistines*, 90–105.

————. *A Note on Literary Criticism*. New York: Vanguard Press, 1936.

Gertsfelde, V. "A Communist on Joyce," *Living Age* 347 (November 1934): 268–70.

Gilbert, Stuart. *James Joyce's "Ulysses"*. 1930. Reprint New York: Random House, Vintage Books, 1955.

Givens, Seon, ed. *James Joyce: Two Decades of Criticism*. New York: Vanguard Press, 1963.

Glicksberg, Charles I., ed. *American Literary Criticism 1900–1950*. New York: Hendrick House, 1951.

Gold, Mike. "Notes of the Month." *The New Masses* 6 (September 1930): 4–5.

Graff, Gerald. "American Criticism Left and Right." In *Ideology and Classic American Literature*, edited by Sacvan Bercovitch and Myra Jehlen, 91–124. Cambridge: Cambridge University Press, 1986.

Grattan, C. Hartley, ed. *The Critique of Humanism*. New York: Brewer and Warren, 1930.

Hawthorn, Jeremy. "*Ulysses*, Modernism, and Marxist Criticism." In *James Joyce and Modern Literature*, edited by W.J. McCormack and Alistair Stead, 112–25. London: Routledge and Kegan Paul, 1982.

Herring, Phillip. "Joyce's Politics." In *New Light on Joyce*, edited by Fritz Senn, 3–14. Bloomington: Illinois University Press, 1972.

Hicks, Granville. "The Crisis in American Criticism." 1933. Reprinted in *Granville Hicks in The New Masses*, edited by Jack Alan Robbins, 5–16. Port Washington, New York: Kennikat Press, 1974.

———. "Eliot in Our Time." 1936. Reprinted in *Granville Hicks in The New Masses*, 100–105.

———. "In Defense of James Farrell." 1936. Reprinted in *Granville Hicks in The New Masses*, 106–109.

———. "Literature and Revolution." 1935. Reprinted in Glicksberg, ed., *American Literary Criticism, 1900–1950*, 408–26.

——— et al., eds. *Proletarian Literature in the United States*. London: Laurence and Wishart, 1935.

Hoeveler, J. David. *The New Humanism: A Critique of Modern America*. Charlottesville: University Press of Virginia, 1977.

Houdebine, Jean-Louis. "Jdanov ou Joyce." *Tel Quel* (Spring 1977): 29–49.

Howe, Irving. "Literature and Liberalism." In *Literature and Liberalism*, edited by Edward Zwick, i–xxiii. Washington, D.C.: The New Republic Book Co., 1976.

———. *A Margin of Hope: An Intellectual Biography*. New York: Harcourt, Brace, Jovanovitch, 1982.

Huysmans, Joris K. *Against the Grain*. New York: Dover Publication, Inc., 1969.

Hynes, Sam. "Catholicism of James Joyce." *Commonweal*, (22 Feb. 1952): 487–489.

Jauss, Hans Robert. *Towards an Aesthetic of Reception*. Minneapolis: University of Minnesota Press, 1982.

Jolas, Eugene. "My Friend James Joyce." 1948. Reprinted in Givens, ed., *James Joyce: Two Decades of Criticism*, 3–18.

Joyce, James. *Dubliners*. New York: Viking, 1967.

———. *Finnegans Wake*. New York: Viking, 1975.

———. *A Portrait of the Artist as a Young Man*. New York: Penguin, 1977.

———. *Ulysses*. New York: Random House, 1961.

Kazin, Alfred. *On Native Grounds*. New York: Harcourt Brace Jovanovich, 1970.

———. *Starting Out in the Thirties*. Boston: Little, Brown, 1962.

Kenner, Hugh. *Dublin's Joyce*. Boston: Beacon, 1956.

———. *Joyce's Voices*. Berkeley and Los Angeles: University of California Press, 1978.

———. "The Pedagogue as Critic." In Young, ed., *The New Criticism and After*, 36–46.

———. *Ulysses*. London: George Allen and Unwin, 1980.

Leavis, F. R. *The Great Tradition*. New York: New York University Press, 1973.

Levin, Harry. *James Joyce: A Critical Introduction*. 2d Edition. Norfolk, Conn.: New Directions, 1960.

Lewis, Wyndham. "An Analysis of the Mind of James Joyce." In *Time and Western Man*. 1927. Reprint Boston: Beacon Press, 1957, 75–113.

Libo, Zhou. *Sanshi Niandai Wenxue Pinlun Ji*. Shanghai: Literature and Art Publishing House, 1984.

Litz, A. Walton. "*Ulysses* and Its Audience." In *James Joyce: The Centennial Symposium*, edited by Morris Beja et al., 220–30. Urbana: University of Illinois Press, 1986.

Lukacs, Georg. *The Meaning of Contemporary Realism*. London: Merlin Press, 1962.

———. *Realism in Our Time: Literature and the Class Struggle*. New York: Harper and Row, 1964.

Macdonald, Dwight. "Kulturbolschewismus Is Here." *Partisan Review* 8 (Nov.–Dec. 1941): 442–451.

MacLeish, Archibald. *The Irresponsibles*. New York: Duell, Sloan, and Pearce, 1940.

———. *Letters of Archibald MacLeish, 1907–1982*. Edited by R. H. Winnick. Boston: Houghton Mifflin, 1983.

———. "Post-War Writers and Pre-War Readers." *New Republic* 102 (June 10, 1940): 789–90.

———. Review of *The First World War*, edited by Laurence Stallings. *New Republic* 76 (Sept. 20, 1933): 159–60.

———. *A Time to Act*. Boston: Houghton Mifflin, 1943.

———. *A Time to Speak*. Boston: Houghton Mifflin, 1940.

Maltz, Albert. "What Shall We Ask of Writers?" *New Masses* 58 (Feb. 12, 1946): 19–22.

Manganiello, Dominic. *Joyce's Politics*. London: Routledge and Kegan Paul, 1980.

Meyers, Jeffrey. *The Enemy: A Biography of Wyndham Lewis*. London: Routledge and Kegan Paul, 1980.

Miller-Budnitskaya, R. "James Joyce's *Ulysses*." *Dialectics* 5 (1938): 6–26.

Mirsky, D. P. "Joyce and Irish Literature." *New Masses* 10–11 (April 3, 1934): 31–34.

More, Paul Elmer. "The Demon of the Absolute." 1928. Reprinted in Glicksberg, ed., *American Literary Criticism 1900–1950*, 258–87.

———. *On Being Human*. Princeton: Princeton University Press, 1936.

Moretti, Franco. *Signs Taken for Wonders: Essays in the Sociology of Literary Forms*. Great Britain: The Thetford Press, 1983.

Morse, J. Mitchell. *The Sympathetic Alien: James Joyce and Catholicism*. New York: New York University Press, 1959.

Moscato, Michael and LeBlanc, Leslie, eds. *The United States of America v. One Book Entitled "Ulysses" by James Joyce*. Frederick, Md: University Publications of America, 1984.

Muir, Edwin. *Transition: Essays on Contemporary Literature*. London: Hogarth Press, 1926.

Nelson, Raymond. *Van Wyck Brooks: A Writer's Life*. New York: E. P. Dutton, 1981.

Noon, William T., S.J. *Joyce and Aquinas*. New Haven: Yale University Press, 1957.

O'Brien, Conor Cruise. "Passion and Cunning: An Essay on the Politics of W.B. Yeats." In *In Excited Reverie*, edited by A Norman Jeffares and K. G. Cross, 207–78. New York: Macmillan, 1965.

"On the Brooks-MacLeish Thesis." *Partisan Review* 9 (Jan.–Feb. 1942): 38–47.

Peake, C. H. *James Joyce: The Citizen and the Artist*. Stanford: Stanford University Press, 1977.

Pinto, Vivian de Sola. *The Politics of Twentieth Century Novelists*. New York: Hawthorne, 1971.

Poggioli, Renato. *The Theory of the Avant-Garde*. Cambridge: Harvard University Press. 1968.

Poirier, Richard. *The Renewal of Literature*. New York: Random House, 1987.

Radek, Karl. "James Joyce or Socialist Realism?" In Zhdanov et al, eds., *Problems of Soviet Literature*, 150–82.

Rahv, Philip. "An Aesthetic of Migration." Review of *The Destructive Element*, by Stephen Spender. *Partisan Review* 3 (April 1936): 28–29.

———. *Essays on Literature and Politics, 1932–1972.* Edited by Arabel J. Porter and Andrew J. Dvosin. Boston: Houghton Mifflin, 1978.

———. "How the Wasteland Became a Flower Garden." *Partisan Review* 1 (Sept.–Oct. 1934): 37–42.

———. "Proletarian Literature: A Political Autopsy." 1939. Reprinted in *Essays on Literature and Politics, 1932–1972,* 292–308.

———, and Wallace Phelps [William Phillips]. "Problems and Perspectives in Revolutionary Literature." *Partisan Review* 1 (June–July, 1934): 3–22.

Ransom, John Crowe. "The Aesthetic of *Finnegans Wake.*" *Kenyon Review* 1 (Autumn, 1939): 424–428.

———. "Criticism, Inc." 1938. Reprinted in Glicksberg, ed., *American Literary Criticism, 1900–1950,* 453–467.

———. "Modern with the Southern Accent." *Virginia Quarterly Review,* April 1935, 184–193.

———. "Reconstructed But Unregenerate." In Davidson et al., *I'll Take My Stand: The South and the Agrarian Tradition.*

———. "T. S. Eliot: The Historical Critic." In *The New Criticism,* 135–210. Norfolk, Ct.: New Directions, 1941.

Read, Forrest, ed. *Pound/Joyce.* New York: New Directions, 1967.

Rideout, Walter. *The Radical Novel in the United States, 1900–1954.* Cambridge: Harvard University Press, 1956.

Schlauch, Margaret. "The Language of James Joyce." *Science and Society* 3 (Fall 1939): 482–97.

Scholes, Robert. "Joyce and Modernist Ideology." In *Coping with Joyce,* edited by M. Beja and S. Benstock, 91–110. Columbus: Ohio State University Press, 1989.

Schwartz, Delmore. *Selected Essays of Delmore Schwartz.* Edited by Donald A. Dike and David H. Zucker. Chicago: University of Chicago Press, 1970.

Slochower, Harry. "In Quest of Everyman: James Joyce and Eugene O'Neill." In *No Voice Is Wholly Lost.* Kingsway, Eng.: Dennis Dobson, 1946.

Smidt, Kristian. *James Joyce and the Cultic Use of Fiction.* New York: Humanities Press, 1959.

Spender, Stephen. *The Destructive Element.* London: Jonathan Cape, 1935.

Spiller, Robert, ed. *The Van Wyck Brooks–Lewis Mumford Letters.* New York: E.P. Dutton, 1970.

Strong, L.A.G. *The Sacred River: An Approach to James Joyce.* New York: Pellegrini and Cudahy, 1951.

Sullivan, Kevin. *Joyce Among the Jesuits.* New York: Columbia University Press, 1958.

Tate, Allen. "Ezra Pound and the Bollingen Prize." 1949. Reprinted in *Essays of Four Decades*, 509–13. Chicago: The Swallow Press, 1968.

———. "The Profession of Letters in the South." 1935. Reprinted in *Essays of Four Decades*, 517–34.

———. *Reason in Madness: Critical Essays.* New York: G. P. Putnam's Sons, 1935.

———. "To Whom Is the Poet Responsible?" 1951. Reprinted in *Essays of Four Decades*, 17–29.

———, and Caroline Gordon, eds. *The House of Fiction.* 2d edition. New York: Charles Scribner's, 1960.

Trilling, Lionel. "Freud and Literature." 1940. Reprinted in revised form in *The Liberal Imagination*, 34–57.

———. "James Joyce in His Letters." 1968. Reprinted in Chace, ed., *Joyce: A Collection of Critical Essays*, 143–65.

———. *The Liberal Imagination.* New York: Viking, 1950.

Trotsky, Leon. *Literature and Revolution.* New York: Russell and Russell, 1957.

———. *Leon Trotsky on Literature and Art.* Edited by Paul Siegel. New York: Pathfinder Press, 1970.

Ussher, Arland. *Three Great Irishmen: Shaw, Yeats, Joyce.* New York: Devin-Adair, 1953.

Wain, John, ed. *Edmund Wilson: The Man and His Work.* New York: New York University Press, 1978.

Wald, Alan. *James T. Farrell: The Revolutionary Socialist Years.* New York: New York University Press, 1978.

Wasserstrom, William. *The Legacy of Van Wyck Brooks.* Carbondale: Southern Illinois University Press, 1971.

Watson, G.J. "The Politics of Ulysses." In *Joyce's Ulysses: The Larger Perspective*, edited by Fritz Senn, 39–58. Newark: University of Delaware Press, 1987.

West, Alick. "James Joyce: *Ulysses.*" In *Crisis and Criticism*, 143–180. London: Laurence and Wishart, 1935.

Whitfield, Stephen J. *A Critical American: The Politics of Dwight Macdonald.* Hamden, Conn.: Archon Books, 1984.

Wilson, Edmund. "Archibald MacLeish and 'the Word.'" *New Republic* 103 (July 1, 1940): 30–32.

———. *Axel's Castle.* New York: Scribner's, 1931.

———. "H.C. Earwicker and Family." *New Republic* 99 (June 28, 1939): 203–6.

———. *Letters on Literature and Politics, 1912–1972*. Edited by Elena Wilson. New York: Farrar, Straus, and Giroux, 1977.

———. "Marxism and Literature." In *The Triple Thinkers: Ten Essays on Literature*, 266–89. New York: Harcourt, Brace, 1938.

———. "Mr. Brooks's Second Phase." *New Republic* 103 (Sept. 30, 1940): 52–54.

———. "Mr. More and the Mithraic Bull." 1937. Reprinted in *The Triple Thinkers*, 11–21.

———. "Notes on Babbitt and More." In Grattan, ed., *The Critique of Humanism*, 39–62.

———. *The Triple Thinkers*. New York: Harcourt, Brace, 1938.

———. "*Ulysses.*" *New Republic* 31 (July 5, 1922): 164–66.

———. *The Wound and the Bow*. Cambridge, Mass.: Riverside Press, 1941.

Woolf, Virginia. *The Common Reader*. New York: Harcourt, Brace and World, 1948.

Young, Thomas Daniel, ed. *The New Criticism and After*. Charlottesville: University Press of Virginia, 1976.

Zhantieva, B. G. "Joyce's *Ulysses.*" 1965. Reprinted in *Preserve and Create*, edited by Ursula Beitz and Gaylord C. LeRoy, 138–73. New York: Humanities Press, 1973.

Zhdanov, Andrey A. *Essays on Literature, Philosophy, and Music*. New York: International Publishers, 1950.

———. "Soviet Literature—The Richest in Ideas, The Most Advanced Literature." In Zhdanov et al. eds., *Problems of Soviet Literature*, 15–24.

——— et al, eds. *Problems of Soviet Literature: Reports and Speeches of the First Soviet Writers' Congress*. New York: International Publishers, 1935.

Index

Aaron, Daniel, 21, 64
Adams, R. M., 6, 26
Agrarians, Southern (see also New
  Critics): 62, 116–19, 128
Aquinas, St. Thomas, 163
Auden, W. H., 67, 78

Babbitt, Irving (see also New
  Humanists): 52–55, 60, 88, 131
Balzac, Honoré de, 28
Barrett, William, 83
Baudelaire, Charles, 5, 18
Beach, Sylvia, 63
Beckett, Samuel, 135
Blackmur, R. P., 60, 78, 115, 125; on
  Ulysses, 131–34
Blake, William, 158, 165
Bloom, Leopold, 14, 59, 80, 106,
  144–45; Kenner, Ellmann dispute
  over, 150, 153, 179–81; Marxists
  on, 33–35, 45; New Critics on,
  124, 127–28, 133, 135; Wilson on,
  93, 99–100
Bloom, Molly, 111, 158; Ellmann on,
  180–81; Kenner on, 153–54; Marx-
  ists on, 31–32; New Critics on,
  124, 127; Wilson on, 55–56, 93,
  99–100
Boyle, Robert, S. J., 138, 140, 160,
  162–64, 167
Brooks, Cleanth, 78, 116, 125–28

Brooks, Van Wyck, 8, 40, 44, 48, 50,
  63, 68–75, 77–78, 88–89, 122–23,
  191–92
Brown, Richard, 5–6, 184
Bruno, Giordano, 31
Budgen, Frank, 138
Burke, Kenneth, 60

Calmer, Alan, 88
Catholic critics (see also Boyle, Ken-
  ner, Morse, Noon, Smidt, Sulli-
  van, Strong): 59, 133, 172; Joyce as
  problem for, 137–42
Chace, William M., 13, 16, 18, 83,
  109, 111–12
Chekhov, Anton, 184
Colum, Mary, 137
Communism, appeal of in U.S., 21–
  22
Communist Party, U.S., 21, 24, 37,
  63, 91, 189
Congress of Soviet Writers, 23, 81
Cowley, Malcolm, 11, 15–16, 22,
  39–44, 60, 75, 90, 105, 131, 189
Curtius, E. R., 173

Dante, 165, 180
Dedalus, Stephen (see also *A Portrait
  of the Artist as a Young Man*): 59–60,
  66, 90, 93, 151–54, 180, 186–87;
  Catholic critics on, 56, 160, 162,

205

Compositor: Asco Trade Typesetting Ltd., Hong Kong
Text: 11/13 Bembo
Display: Bembo
Printer and Binder: Thomson-Shore, Inc.

DEMCO